# THE AUTHOR

Rosemary Conley entered the slimming business 17 years ago when she founded the SAGG Slimming and Good Grooming Organization. Eight years later she sold the business to IPC Magazines Ltd and was appointed Managing Director of the nationwide Successful Slimming Clubs – a position she held for 5 years until deciding to go freelance once more.

During her time with IPC Rosemary also scripted two highly successful Slimobility exercise cassettes and wrote three books – *Eat Yourself Slim*, *Eat And Stay Slim* and *Positive Living*.

It was immediately after she went freelance that Rosemary discovered her extraordinary new diet. A gall bladder crisis set her on the road to discovering that very low fat eating could knock inches off the hips and thighs. As a result Rosemary Conley's Hip and Thigh Diet was published in 1988 and became the number one bestseller of the year. Following the success of the book in the UK an Australian and New Zealand edition was published in the autumn. Following her promotional tour 'down-under' the book rocketed to number one in both countries.

Rosemary has devised and produced a Hip and Thigh exercise cassette and video and is an accomplished and experienced broadcaster on both national and international TV and radio. She is a regular contributor on the ITV series 'Look Good, Feel Great!' produced by Central Television and teaches weekly slimming and exercise classes at the Holiday Inn in Leicester and at her home.

The success of the *Hip and Thigh Diet* has led to the formation of Rosemary Conley Enterprises. Rosemary's husband, Mike Rimmington, has joined her in the business, running the merchandising division.

Both Rosemary and Mike are born-again Christians. Rosemary has a daughter, Dawn, by her first marriage.

*Also in Arrow by Rosemary Conley*

EAT YOURSELF SLIM
EAT AND STAY SLIM
POSITIVE LIVING
ROSEMARY CONLEY'S HIP AND THIGH DIET
ROSEMARY CONLEY'S INCH LOSS PLAN

# Rosemary Conley's
# COMPLETE HIP AND THIGH DIET

ARROW BOOKS

Arrow Books Limited
20 Vauxhall Bridge Road, London SW1V 2SA

An imprint of Random Century Group

London Melbourne Sydney Auckland
Johannesburg and agencies throughout
the world

First published 1989
Reprinted 1989 (twelve times)
Reprinted 1990 (three times)

© Rosemary Conley 1989

This book is sold subject to the condition that it shall not, by way of trade or otherwise, be lent, resold, hired out, or otherwise circulated without the publisher's prior consent in any form of binding or cover other than that in which it is published and without a similar condition including this condition being imposed on the subsequent purchaser

Printed and bound in Great Britain by
Courier International Ltd, Tiptree, Essex

ISBN 0 09 963710 3

# Contents

| | | |
|---|---|---|
| | Acknowledgements | 7 |
| | Introduction | 9 |
| | Measurement Record Charts | 13 |
| 1 | 'It works! It really, really works!' | 17 |
| 2 | Binge no more! | 23 |
| 3 | 'Yes – this diet really *does* slim hips and thighs!' | 28 |
| 4 | The 'Tum and Bum Diet' for men | 50 |
| 5 | Eat your way to better health | 58 |
| 6 | 'This diet changed my life' | 88 |
| 7 | Thighs of relief – Hip, Hip, Hooray! | 96 |
| 8 | The Diet – extended version | 105 |
| 9 | Recipes | 137 |
| 10 | Exercise, massage creams, treatments . . . Do they help? | 199 |
| 11 | The Maintenance Programme | 209 |
| 12 | Living life to the full | 232 |
| 13 | A guide to fat in food – the complete tables | 235 |
| | Extra help is available – exercise cassette, video and postal slimming course | 285 |

# Acknowledgements

I would like to acknowledge with grateful thanks the readers and followers of my first *Hip and Thigh Diet* who kindly wrote so many wonderful letters telling me of their success on the diet, and to those who so thoughtfully completed questionnaires, giving me a great deal of valuable information. I am also very grateful to those who submitted recipes. Without all these wonderful people this book would not have been written.

I would like to thank JVF Consultants Ltd whose computer proved invaluable in reproducing the data from the questionnaires and preparing the tables of fat content in foods. Without their help I could not have completed the book on time. Also, I owe my thanks to my publishers, Arrow Books, for their help, co-operation and support throughout, and to Lewis Mantus of Media Angles Ltd for organizing such a splendidly successful promotional tour for the first *Hip and Thigh Diet* book. Special thanks must go to my secretary, Diane, not only for her endless hours of typing, but also for her thoughtfulness and total co-operation. And to my dear husband Mike for his unfaltering love, co-operation and encouragement throughout the many weeks I spent scribbling away at this manuscript. Thank you all.

# Introduction

PO Box 4
Mountsorrel
Loughborough
Leicestershire
LE12 7LB

Dear Reader,

This *Complete Hip and Thigh Diet* book has been written as a direct result of the hundreds of letters I received only weeks after publication of my first *Hip and Thigh Diet*.

This incredibly effective diet was discovered completely by accident. I found myself faced with the choice of surgery for gall stones or embarking on a very low fat diet. I opted for the latter and, not only did I avoid the surgeon's knife, but also discovered a side effect of the diet which can only be described as a miracle. My disproportionately pear-shaped body began to change shape. Inches fell off my hips and thighs for the first time in my life! The members of my exercise classes pleaded with me to share the diet with them and, amazingly, they enjoyed the same results – shedding those inches previously impossible to shift.

I further tested the diet with a team of volunteers recruited through local radio stations and 120 men and women followed the diet for an eight-week trial period. It then became obvious that it wasn't just large-hipped figures that benefited. Those with a top-heavy, 'busty', figure lost weight from their busts, and those with a more roly-poly figure lost it from around their tums. I believe this diet is so effective in shedding inches from our body's waste grounds because the body utilises the highly nutritious food, rather than storing it as reserves of fat as is the case with most junk food. In the Department of Health and Social Security's Report 28 on 'Diet and Cardiovascular Disease', it suggests that *everyone* – regardless of weight, sex, age or condition, could benefit from reducing their fat intake by about one third. I read in one book that we only need six grams of fat a day, and yet most people in the Western world consume a daily average of 130 grams. My diet does not stipulate that slimmers eat anywhere near as few as six grams, just considerably less than the average daily intake. On the Maintenance Programme, the fat allowance is increased, although still lower than the amount we have been used to.

Nutritionally we need fat for energy and certain vitamins. Since these fat soluble vitamins can be stored in the body, there is little risk of deficiency for the duration of the diet. I do however recommend that everyone following the diet take a multivitamin tablet each day to make doubly sure that they are eating sufficient vitamins. But when you commence on the

Maintenance Programme, this should not be necessary.

Just three weeks after the first *Hip and Thigh Diet* book was on sale, letters began flooding through my letterbox. Words like 'incredible', 'fantastic', 'staggering', 'amazing' were used to describe the effect of my diet on readers' bodies. 'I've regained my youthful figure after twenty years', 'I just wouldn't have believed it could have happened, let alone so quickly and so easily!' It was truly wonderful to hear how well the diet was working for everyone.

Also, among the many letters I received, there were many requests for more vegetarian menus and packed lunches. Readers also outlined the benefits to their health that this diet brought them. Arthritics enjoyed greater mobility and less pain; heart patients enjoyed real improvements in their condition; many found that digestion improved and symptoms of PMT disappeared. Also, not surprisingly, gall-stone sufferers enjoyed significant relief. Over 80% said they did feel *healthier* on the diet. I felt I had to write another book to pass on this information, and hope, to others. I have extended the diet to cater for all needs, the recipe section includes 100 mouth-watering ideas for low fat meals and snacks and the fat tables show, at a glance, the fat content of hundreds of foods, so you'll learn quickly which foods to avoid when dining out or shopping.

After endless requests, I have also produced an exercise cassette and video. Also, there is a Postal Slimming Course for those who feel they need personal support. I am always interested to hear of people's experiences and success stories after following the diet. If you would like to complete a questionnaire, please write to me, enclosing a stamped-addressed envelope, at the address at the beginning of this letter. I just want to help you achieve the kind of figure you never even dreamed of. Dieting has never been simpler – there's plenty to eat and no calories or units to count, just incredible results to enjoy.

With very best wishes.

P.S. It is important that you check with your doctor before embarking on this or any other diet or exercise routine, particularly if you have a medical condition.

## Measurement Record Chart

| Date | Weight | Bust | Waist | Hips | Widest Part | Top of Thighs L \| R | Above Knees L \| R | Upper Arms L \| R | Comments |
|------|--------|------|-------|------|-------------|---------------------|---------------------|---------------------|----------|
|      |        |      |       |      |             |                     |                     |                     |          |
|      |        |      |       |      |             |                     |                     |                     |          |
|      |        |      |       |      |             |                     |                     |                     |          |
|      |        |      |       |      |             |                     |                     |                     |          |
|      |        |      |       |      |             |                     |                     |                     |          |
|      |        |      |       |      |             |                     |                     |                     |          |
|      |        |      |       |      |             |                     |                     |                     |          |
|      |        |      |       |      |             |                     |                     |                     |          |
|      |        |      |       |      |             |                     |                     |                     |          |

## Measurement Record Chart

| Date | Weight | Bust | Waist | Hips | Widest Part | Top of Thighs L \| R | Above Knees L \| R | Upper Arms L \| R | Comments |
|------|--------|------|-------|------|-------------|----------------------|--------------------|-------------------|----------|
|      |        |      |       |      |             |                      |                    |                   |          |
|      |        |      |       |      |             |                      |                    |                   |          |
|      |        |      |       |      |             |                      |                    |                   |          |
|      |        |      |       |      |             |                      |                    |                   |          |
|      |        |      |       |      |             |                      |                    |                   |          |
|      |        |      |       |      |             |                      |                    |                   |          |
|      |        |      |       |      |             |                      |                    |                   |          |
|      |        |      |       |      |             |                      |                    |                   |          |
|      |        |      |       |      |             |                      |                    |                   |          |

## Measurement Record Chart

| Date | Weight | Bust | Waist | Hips | Widest Part | Top of Thighs L R | Above Knees L R | Upper Arms L R | Comments |
|---|---|---|---|---|---|---|---|---|---|
| | | | | | | | | | |
| | | | | | | | | | |
| | | | | | | | | | |
| | | | | | | | | | |
| | | | | | | | | | |
| | | | | | | | | | |
| | | | | | | | | | |
| | | | | | | | | | |
| | | | | | | | | | |

## Measurement Record Chart

| Date | Weight | Bust | Waist | Hips | Widest Part | Top of Thighs L \| R | Above Knees L \| R | Upper Arms L \| R | Comments |
|------|--------|------|-------|------|-------------|----------------------|---------------------|--------------------|----------|
|      |        |      |       |      |             |                      |                     |                    |          |
|      |        |      |       |      |             |                      |                     |                    |          |
|      |        |      |       |      |             |                      |                     |                    |          |
|      |        |      |       |      |             |                      |                     |                    |          |
|      |        |      |       |      |             |                      |                     |                    |          |
|      |        |      |       |      |             |                      |                     |                    |          |
|      |        |      |       |      |             |                      |                     |                    |          |
|      |        |      |       |      |             |                      |                     |                    |          |
|      |        |      |       |      |             |                      |                     |                    |          |

# 1
## 'It works! It really, really works!'

'Thanks a million. It works! It really, really works!' read the letter from Lorna Cowley, just one of many I received shortly after the publication of my *Hip and Thigh Diet* in January 1988. Cynthia Wall wrote, 'I never thought I'd be writing to anyone saying "your diet is wonderful" but it is, and I am!' Lorna's letter continued, 'Prior to your book, which I ordered for 21 January, I was 38–34–42 (96–86–107 cm) and 11½ stone (73 kg) and quite despairing of ever being rid of an elephant rear and bulging tummy. By 31 January I could not stop admiring my new image in the long mirror! I was then 38–32–39½ (96–81–100 cm) and 11 stone (70 kg). My engagement ring I have been unable to wear for years; to my delight it fitted with ease last week! Just for curiosity the same day, I put on my swimsuit and I was staggered at the 'New Look' me. Audrey Bewley from North Yorkshire wrote, 'I have been following your Hip and Thigh Diet and every word is true – the weight has gone from the most stubborn parts of my body. I truly love the diet.'

*I knew* my diet worked. It had worked for me and it had left me in no doubt as to its effectiveness when my original trial team put it to the test. The results really were staggering. When the *Sunday Express* bought the serial rights to my book I was terribly excited. I never once doubted my diet's effectiveness but I knew it was not easy to convince the media. *This* diet was different. *This* one worked. *This* one was easy to follow. *This* one made you feel good – not irritable like most diets. And, yes, it really *did* reduce inches around those parts other diets didn't reach.

'Why hasn't anyone discovered the diet before?' I was asked many times during my promotional tour for the book. Funnily enough this type of diet *had* in fact worked before for others but they hadn't realized what was happening to their bodies. I was in an ideal situation, with all the circumstances just presenting themselves perfectly. Let me explain. In 1986, I was struck down with a gall bladder problem and faced imminent surgery. As I was just winding up a business and about to become self-employed I couldn't possibly take six weeks off to have my gall bladder removed. My only way of avoiding surgery was to follow a virtually fat-free diet. I was very determined so I did it! In my job as a slimming and exercise teacher I needed to wear skin-tight leotards and tights. At 5 ft 2 ins (1.57 m) I was not really overweight at 8 st 7 lbs (54 kg) but my enormous posterior and thunder thighs did make me look much weightier than I really was. Consequently, when these embarrassing areas began to slim down, but the rest of me stayed the same, my exercise students became inquisitive – anxious that I should pass on my secret for their benefit! This I did and, yes, it worked for them too.

As I had already had several books published on the subjects of slimming, exercise and positive attitude, it seemed obvious that I should publish a book describing my new miracle eating plan. I realized that to convince the world at large (and my publisher) that my new diet worked, I would have to have detailed information on its success rate. As a regular broadcaster on local radio I asked listeners to try out the diet. They did and it worked for them too. In fact 89% said they lost weight from the areas they particularly wanted to slim. It was so exciting to hear their comments, to see their diminishing measurements, to read how well they felt and how they never felt hungry. I just couldn't believe how positive everyone felt. It was wonderful.

My publisher was as excited as I was. Contracts were hastily drawn up and agreed, and four months later I had finished the book. I can remember posting it by registered post and thinking to myself – I *know* this is going to be a bestseller.

Two weeks after publication my book entered the non-fiction paperback bestseller chart – at number 1. I just couldn't believe it! It stayed there for the next week – dropped to 2, then 3, then up to 1 again where it stayed for over 6 months. The publishers kept reprinting and the readers succeeded in losing their weight and inches and telling their friends.

After about a month I began receiving letters – lots and lots of very encouraging letters. The readers were saying they just couldn't believe that the diet was in fact working just as I had said it would. They couldn't believe the change in their shape. They couldn't believe that this diet worked even though they seemed to be eating much more food than normal. It was their total shock at its effectiveness that prompted them to write. Here are some extracts from their letters.

Jo Higham wrote:

'Dear Rosemary,

I just had to write to you – I am so pleased. I read in the *Sunday Express* about your low fat diet. I followed it – the inches are dropping off!

I am 50 years old. I never sit around. I am basically slim until you get from 3 inches (8 cm) below the waist to halfway down my thighs.

I had four children in four years and ended up with jodhpur thighs. I've dieted, exercised, the lot, and lost weight from my face, bust – never the bum. I've always hated my shape, longed to wear trousers, would love to join keep-fit classes but wouldn't want anyone to see me. I love the sun – but I always need a sheltered spot away from people on the beach! I sit out in my own garden always with a cotton dressing gown ready to wrap around me if anyone comes. I can't wear straight skirts.

Early this winter I emptied my wardrobe and decided my hips were big and I would dress to hide. Lots of black skirts. This year I would stick to sunbathing in sun dresses. Then your article in the paper – I'm overjoyed! I was a chocoholic and I haven't touched a "sinful" thing in eight weeks and it shows.

I just had to tell you I'm so thrilled. I didn't measure myself but I know what I was – I have lost 3 ins (8 cm) from my hips, 3 ins (8 cm) from my widest part and 'a lot' from my thighs. I have lost 1 st 3 lbs (7.7 kg) but from the right place. Last year I had considered the op but it was £1700 and they only took off a litre of fat from each thigh – I didn't think that would even be noticeable. Thanks.'

Two weeks later Jo wrote again in reply to my request for permission to reproduce her letter. This is what she said:

'You have my permission to quote anything from my letter and give my name. I'm so delighted with the diet – I am now down to 8 st 13 lbs (56.8 kg) – never have I ever got to the 8s (below 57 kg). With lots of efforts over the years 9 st 4 lbs (59 kg) was the best I could ever manage. I am just so thrilled: my widest part now is 41 ins (104 cm) – it was going over 45 ins (114 cm) when I started. I'm aiming now to wear trousers on my holidays. I've never worn them since I was a young teenager.'

By now I had designed a questionnaire so I sent one to Jo. It made wonderful reading when it was returned. Jo now had a 35–25–37½ (89–63–95 cm) figure! She had lost more weight and at 5 ft 2½ ins (1.59 m) was now beautifully slim. She wrote:

'I have dropped from 10 st 5 lbs (66 kg) to 8 st 9 lbs (55 kg). I have never been below 9 st (57 kg) for over 20 years. In fact it's been so easy. I began to worry in case I was losing weight because I had some serious illness and not the diet! Everyone remarks on my loss of weight. It has all gone from my bottom.

I must tell you my hope was to get into trousers. This I have done and yesterday I bought some shorts! You've no idea what an achievement this is for me.'

Mrs D. Taylor from Kent wrote:

'Dear Rosemary,

I am just writing to tell you that I am in my seventh week of your Hip and Thigh Diet and already I have lost a stone (6.4 kg) in weight. My shape has returned, my cellulite has virtually disappeared, and as an added bonus I have never felt so fit and well for years.

I have recommended your book to countless people and they in turn are thrilled with the result of their efforts. I am enjoying all the meals and whereas before I used to tuck into toffees and biscuits, I find that I do not miss them at all.'

In reply to my letter asking to reproduce her letter, Mrs Taylor continued:

'Since writing to you I have reached my ideal weight and am now on the maintenance diet, isn't that wonderful!'

# 2
# Binge no more!

The letters I received told me a great deal. Obviously it was wonderful to hear how well everyone was succeeding, but some letters asked for an explanation on certain points. I realized I should have stated that my list of Daily Nutritional Requirements were in fact minimum quantities. I also realized I should have explained more fully why some portion sizes were not stated. I hadn't catered sufficiently for vegetarians and there were too few snack menus for packed lunches. A follow-up book was definitely needed.

In the previous book I deliberately wanted to avoid stating quantities of foods except those which contained fat, e.g. chicken, fish, meat. Fruit and vegetables are offered freely in the hope that slimmers will fill themselves and satisfy their hunger at the same time as breaking that *negative* habit of counting calories. I believe calorie counting leads to binge eating. We are able to cope with a restricted diet for most of the day, but four o'clock arrives, we've munched our way through most of our daily allowance and the prospect of a slim-line evening is just too much. We nibble a little to start with, then it turns into a wholesale binge. We throw in the towel and say, 'Oh well, I'll start properly tomorrow!'

I used to binge terribly – I still do a little, but now only *very* occasionally. Since I have followed my very low fat diet I find I can eat such a volume of food, I don't feel as deprived as I used to when dieting previously. So the fact that I don't specify how big that jacket potato should be is quite deliberate. If having a 12 oz (350 g) potato (which is quite big) means you won't have a binge later, eat it and enjoy it. After a while you will find that as you are allowed one every day if you wish, you don't really *need* such a big one. Gradually you will find yourself selecting food portions much more sensibly. You will feel more relaxed about eating. Your confidence in your will power will gradually increase and you will feel much better about yourself. The same rule applies to your portion of rice or pasta. Eat enough to satisfy yourself.

There is nothing more negative for someone who is trying to reduce their weight than getting up from the table feeling not quite full. If you do this, you will feel deprived and are most at risk to temptation. I usually cook extra vegetables so that I can fill myself up with them if I'm still feeling peckish.

I have an enormous appetite which constantly shocks those who eat with me. I eat as much as most men and when you realize I am quite small at 5 ft 2 ins (1.57 m) I am living proof that this diet *does* work. One word of warning here – if your progress on my diet is really too slow, it is likely to be your portion size that is to blame, so bear this in mind.

Comments made by readers in their lovely letters

to me suggested that they had been able to change their previous bad eating habits completely since following my diet. I wanted to know exactly why this was so, and my comprehensive questionnaire was offered to anyone interested in giving me more details of their progress.

I asked if they had ever binged before following my diet and 70% said they had, whilst the remainder had never done so. I then asked if they had binged at all whilst following the diet and 20.2% said they binged occasionally whilst 77% said they didn't binge at all, 1% said they had continued to binge and the remainder didn't answer the question.

The whole concept of bingeing is quite extraordinary and something that interests me greatly. Bingeing is, I believe, the greatest cause of overweight. Yet most bingeing is done whilst trying to diet! This sounds like a contradiction, but so often someone goes on a diet to lose a few pounds and before they know it they've actually *gained* weight. Just after I was first married I had only 14 lbs (6.4 kg) to lose. I lost 12 (5.4 kg) of them, had a binge, felt cross with myself and panicked – left the slimming group I attended feeling ashamed and in five weeks regained all that I'd lost plus another 14 lbs (6.4 kg)! How often has that happened to slimmers? Millions of times – all because they felt so deprived whilst following the diet. So why did the vast majority of those following my Hip and Thigh Diet *not* binge?

Of those who completed my questionnaire, 63.6% felt their success on this diet, compared with previous diet failures, was attributable to the fact that they could eat so much more on this diet.

I asked my volunteers what they considered were

the most enjoyable aspects of my diet. I offered ten options plus space for additions and asked them to award marks from 1 to 10 in order of preference, marking their favourite aspect with 1 point, and their least favourite with 10.

This was the result, in order of preference:

1. Plenty to eat.
2. No calorie counting.
3. Freedom of choice of menus.
4. No weighing of food.
5. Having three meals a day.
6. Eating as many vegetables as I liked.
7. Eating potatoes.
8. Eating bread.
9. Eating lots of fruit.
10. Having a three-course dinner.

So it is clear to see that lack of hunger and the plain simplicity of the diet were the keys to its success.

Armed with this information, we can now think logically about when we normally binge. I believe we wage a personal war between ourselves and a diet. We feel hungry and a normal slimming diet says 'Too bad, you've had your calories – tough!'

We say, 'I don't want to feel hungry. Why should I feel hungry? Blow it, I'm going to eat and I'm going to eat what I want!' And off we go for the highest calorie food we can get our teeth into. In fact, it becomes almost like a race to see how much food we can ram down before the diet 'claps us in irons' again. During a binge we really want to make the most of it – sultanas, raisins out of the baking cupboard, ice cream out of the freezer, cheese from the refrigerator, bread and jam, biscuits (even the ones we don't like) – *anything*! We never think, 'I'll have egg and chips', because that would take too long. We want food *now*. Also, we think we're only going to have just this little ... but it's never a 'little' anything, because it's a nasty, deceptive, slippery slope which we tumble down, faster and faster, away from all reason or common sense. We are often not truly conscious of what we are doing. Afterwards we are furious with ourselves. If you've ever binged – you know what I mean.

So, avoiding binge eating is the key to success if we want to stick to a reducing diet; and want to achieve our goal and stay there!

One reader, Linda Wood, wrote to me, saying:

> 'I am a lot more confident about myself because I know my weight will continue to come off, as I am eating so much more healthily. In fact, I don't feel as though I'm "rushed" on this diet; I feel this diet is a whole new way of eating for me. It certainly works for me, I feel tons better for it, and have lost all my guilty feelings about bingeing.
> 
> I want to say a big thank you.'

This diet does in fact prevent a lot of the feelings of hunger and deprivation which lead to bingeing. And if you can cure bingeing, you can be assured that you'll keep around your ideal weight for ever. As Miss J. W. wrote:

> 'My once regular evening binges seem to have been eradicated for ever as my mental attitude has changed for the better. So thank you for helping me to feel like a spring chicken!'

# 3
# 'Yes – this diet really *does* slim hips and thighs!'

After my own experience of the diet and seeing the results of my initial trial team there was no doubt in my mind that this diet *did* slim hips and thighs. During my promotional tour I was constantly questioned by interviewers as to the *real* effect of the diet. 'But surely you lose weight from problem areas if you slim for long enough anyway,' they would say. Yes, that's true, but you would also lose weight from areas you didn't want to slim, such as your bust.

I was determined to show that my diet *did* work, and I was lucky enough to have plenty of people to back me up. Followers of the diet were so overwhelmed at their success that they wrote telling me their experiences and miraculous inch losses; at every radio phone-in, someone rang in to say how brilliantly the diet had worked for them – losing inches exactly from where I said they would.

Here are extracts from just a few of the many, many letters I have received:

Nurse Janet Farrar wrote:

'Not only have I been impressed with this diet and its results; my colleagues (I am a nurse) have been so amazed that many of them have followed the diet, also with surprising results.

I have been teaching dance and exercise classes for some years, and in spite of all the exercise I do and have done, I have never been able to reduce my enormous thighs significantly – until now. I intend following the diet and maintenance programme and spreading the good word to as many people as possible!
P.S. I am a whole dress size smaller now! Wonderful.'

Jo Hodgart wrote:

'Although I have not lost a great deal of weight I have lost inches, yet virtually none from my bust.'

On previous diets Jo said her bust completely disappeared.

Mrs J. P. N. wrote:

'As you will see from this questionnaire, I could hardly be described as "overweight" being 7 st 9 lbs (49 kg) to begin with. However, I did have pads of fat on my hips which looked like saddlebags which developed during my last pregnancy, over fourteen years ago. I had found this fat impossible to shift, even after practically starving myself at one stage – all I succeeded in losing at that time was my bust! So, when I heard about the Hip and Thigh Diet I decided to give it a go, although I was very sceptical that it would work. You can imagine how I felt when I could almost literally see this very unwanted fat disappearing in front of my eyes. I am delighted with the results. I must be honest and say that I didn't follow this diet to the letter, rather I adapted it to suit myself. There weren't too many three-course dinners for me – I found that simply too filling – but I did stick strictly to a low fat diet, as I discovered which foods contained little or no fat, and I will keep to a low fat diet in the future.'

Mrs Lynne Tindale wrote:

'After the birth of my second baby I seemed to be stuck at 11 stone (70 kg), but after following the Hip and Thigh Diet for eight weeks, I am back to the weight I was before I became pregnant, but now I find that even at my "normal" weight my hips, thighs *and* bottom are much slimmer than I can ever remember – jeans are quite baggy!

I also found that on the diet I even had enough energy to cope with a lively four-year-old boy and my new baby girl.'

Ann Burton wrote to me explaining that all her life she had wanted to lose weight from her hips – 'dieting usually meant losing it from my bust and waist only'. After reading my book she decided to give the diet a whirl. In seven weeks she lost 12 lbs (5.4 kg) and reached her goal.

'I was astonished at the amount of food I was actually eating and only very rarely did I feel hungry between meals. . . . In fact, I don't regard myself as being on a *diet* – I am eating sensibly and healthily. I have lost 2½ ins (10 cm) from my hips and 2½ ins (10 cm) from the top of my thighs.

I can now get into clothes which have always been too tight but, on the other hand, some of my clothes are now too large.'

Joanne Goulding wrote:

'I just thought that I would write and tell you how successful your Hip and Thigh Diet has been for me and to express my thanks to you for developing it.

As I was not really overweight or fat to start with I was quite amazed that I lost weight and in the right places.'

Joanne lost 1 in (2.5 cm) from her bust and waist, 3 ins (7.5 cm) from her hips, 3½ ins (9 cm) from her widest part, 2½ ins (6 cm) from each thigh and 2½ ins (6 cm) from around the top of each knee. At 5 ft 1½ ins (1.56 m) she was delighted to reduce from 8 st 7 lbs (54 kg) to 7 st 12 lbs (50 kg) – ideal for her height.

Valerie Cousins wrote:

'Your Hip and Thigh Diet has completely changed my life. I am only a small person (5 ft 2 ins [1.57 m] in fact) and was not terribly overweight at 9 st 7 lbs (60 kg). I now weigh 8 st 9½ lbs (55 kg). I have been on your diet seven weeks, but am determined to stay on it further. I am told I look years younger and it's all thanks to you. I am so grateful to you . . . I seem to have so much confidence since regaining my teenage figure. Thanks.'

I asked Valerie to complete my questionnaire. By then her weight had reduced to 8 st 7 lbs (54 kg). It was good to see that Valerie had lost nothing from her 32-inch (81 cm) bust, but her waist had reduced by 2 ins (5 cm) to 26 ins (66 cm). Her inch loss from her largest areas – hips and tops of legs – was a wonderful 4½ ins (11 cm) and 4 ins (10 cm) respectively, leaving her with youthful 35½-inch (90 cm) hips. She commented:

'I am now able to put on my jeans; I feel like a teenager again. I have not stopped the diet as I wish to improve my figure further and you have given me the determination to do this. I have no intention of smothering my bread in inches of butter again – I have no wish to. This diet really has become a way of life for me.'

Barbara Jones wrote:

'This diet has produced such a noticeable effect, especially on the hips/thighs, that everyone has commented on it. Lots of people have gone out and bought the book as a result. I feel fitter and healthier and, I have been told, look younger. I have lost weight in proportion and although I am still somewhat overweight (I want to lose another 7 lbs [3.2 kg]), I have gained a balanced figure, which makes me look slimmer. I have previously lost the same amount of weight, which I regained, but have never achieved my present shape. I have never felt the urge to binge or break my diet, although we have still socialized and gone out for meals, so I feel this time it will be easier to maintain my weight.'

Sharon Rice wrote:

'Before starting the diet I was slightly overweight, yet despite working out three times a week at the gym I was unable to shift any weight from my hips or buttocks; especially bad was the pad of fat that had accumulated around the hips and at the back of the hips. The gym instructor said it was the hardest place to shift fat from, but suggested some exercise which I had to do hundreds of "repeats" of. I persevered with the exercises until your book came along, and hey presto! With a combination of the diet and the exercises, the flab started to disappear.

The thing I liked most about the diet was the variety and amounts of food that I could eat. This fitted in perfectly with my weight-training, unlike other diets. I work out strenuously for 1½ hours, three times a week, so on the days that I wasn't training I'd eat "light" selections, i.e. lots of fruit and salad, then on training days when I needed something more filling, I'd opt for the "heavier" selections, i.e. bread, jacket potatoes, baked beans, etc. Following this routine I found the weight came off steadily, and has stayed off.

The other good thing is that although I'm no longer following the diet, I've found my eating habits have changed for the better. I don't miss butter in sandwiches – it's no longer necessary – nor my once-weekly portion of fish and chips – far too fatty. The hardest part is avoiding the "hidden" fats in biscuits, cream crackers, etc., but I am trying to re-educate myself.

My hair and skin have improved no end.'

Lynn Cook wrote:

'I now weigh 10 st 2 lbs (64.5 kg) and miraculously the weight has gone from all the right places. I have lost 2½ ins (6 cm) from my hips and 1½ ins (3.8 cm) from each thigh and 1 inch (2.5 cm) from my waist. When I have tried to diet in the past by counting calories, the weight was lost from the wrong areas and I didn't find the amount of food allowed satisfying enough. On your diet I am rarely hungry and find that I really enjoy the food.'

The following week Lynn completed a questionnaire, by which time she had lost another 2 lbs (1 kg) – making her loss 12 lbs (5.4 kg) in seven weeks. Her hips had slimmed still further from 41 ins (104 cm) to 38 ins (97 cm), her widest part from 42 ins (106 cm) to 39 ins (99 cm). She had only lost 1 inch (2.5 cm) off her bust, reducing it to 34 inches (86 cm). She summed up by saying:

'I think this diet has revolutionized my eating habits and I will be able to follow the maintenance diet permanently (with the occasional lapse such as when eating out, which I don't need to feel guilty about).'

How important that last comment is: don't feel guilty when you do dine out.

Janet Lea wrote:

'I would like to say a very big thank you for giving me the inspiration to do something about my shape. I have always had a very definite pear shape throughout my life, and a big bottom which has always made me most unhappy; and I have always tried to excrcise/diet in order to lose this shape. Although I have never been exactly overweight, I always found difficulty in buying clothes and remained a pear shape with a lot of cellulite around my thighs which was most unsightly in either shorts or bathing costumes. As I got older (I am 42) I found it increasingly difficult to diet and very often when trying to reduce my calorie intake, found I felt quite nauseous and not able to continue a diet for more than a couple of days. In fact over the past three or four years I had found it impossible to follow any diet at all, and had resigned myself to accepting I would always be pear-shaped.

I read an article on Rosemary Conley and was inspired by what appeared to be a kindred spirit. I thought I would give this diet my once-and-for-all best shot. To my surprise I found it easy to follow, most enjoyable, and was not hungry at all. Friends and colleagues at work were amazed at the loss of weight from my waist and hips as my shape had been a source of much comment – and indeed I still have difficulty in accepting that I am a slim size 12 as opposed to a lumpy 14. Friends are constantly remarking on my new shape.

Because I have a job as a secretary which naturally means sitting down a lot, I am amazed at how the cellulite has gone. My thighs are quite smooth in comparison to before and I would not now hesitate to wear shorts or a swimming costume without constantly pulling down the legs to hide my lumpy thighs. I feel and look more attractive and I am very happy with my new shape.'

Janet lost 17 lbs (7.7 kg) in eight weeks, and lost 2 ins (5 cm) from her bust, 4 ins (10 cm) from her waist and hips, and 2½ ins (6 cm) from each thigh.

Veronica Jarvis wrote:

'I have felt so well and already can see how the inches are disappearing. Before I felt bloated and had no energy but now, even after a hard day, I no longer feel worn out. My thighs have always been like tree trunks and have never responded to any other diet I've tried. Although I would dearly love to lose more from that area, they do look a better shape.'

As I was reading through my manuscript of this book before delivering it to my publishers, I received a questionnaire from Mary Hamilton and I just had to include her comments and statistical information because they were so good.

Mary lost 34 lbs (15.4 kg) in 14 weeks, she is 5 ft 2 ins (1.57 m) tall and now weighs 9 st 10 lbs (61.8 kg). She lost 2½ ins (6 cm) from her bust, 4 ins (10 cm) from waist, her hips and widest part, 2½ ins (6 cm) from her left thigh and 3½ ins (9 cm) from her right one. This is what Mary wrote on the back of her questionnaire:

'Ever since I had my tonsils out at the age of five, I have been fat. My lightest weight ever was 9½ st (60.4 kg). My heaviest was 11½ st (73.2 kg). That was when I tried your diet. My thighs were really enormous – in fact my husband used to say that if he could breed pigs with legs like mine he would make a fortune! Today is 26 June and I am down to 9½ st (60.4 kg) which is where I started from. Altogether, I have lost 2 st (12.8 kg) on this diet even though I have occasionally cheated. My thighs are still a bit heavy although I can now wear trousers without looking totally ridiculous. My aim is to reach 8½ st (54 kg) or possibly 8 st (51 kg) by which time my thighs should be normal – I hope.

The best thing is when people say to me, "You've lost some weight, haven't you." I feel very proud of what I've done. All the jokes about not stepping off high pavements because I'll bang my bottom are a thing of the past, thanks to your diet. Let's hope I can carry on and lose another stone (6.4 kg). Who knows, even I might get into a pair of size 10 slimfit jeans.'

By asking readers to complete the questionnaire I was able to see clearly the evidence of inch loss from normally stubborn areas. And I received answers to many other useful questions.

*An incredible 95% said they were surprised with their inch losses achieved on my diet.* I asked the question, 'What was your reaction after following the Hip and Thigh Diet?' Nearly half (46.8%) were 'amazed', almost a third (31%) were 'pleasantly surprised' whilst all of the remainder (22.2%) felt 'satisfied'. *None* were disappointed.

The league table of parts of the body to reduce most significantly is as follows (some dieters ticked more than one area):

| | |
|---|---|
| Hips | 69% |
| Waist | 45.6% |
| Thighs | 43.3% |
| Tummy | 33.9% |
| Bust | 16.4% |
| Other | 5.3% |
| Knees | 4.7% |
| Arms | 3.5% |

By any stretch of the imagination this was a pretty staggering result. These figures were even better than those from my previous trial. As the diet detailed in the book was considerably extended from its original trial form it gave the slimmers more choice and accordingly a much greater degree of success.

It was interesting that, of the 16.4% who lost most inches off their bust, 15% did actually say in the questionnaire that they *wanted* to reduce in this area, leaving only 1.4% of the total who lost significantly from their bust and didn't wish to.

The statistics from the returned questionnaires were computerized, enabling me to see average inch losses across the board. In arriving at the following set of figures no consideration was taken as to whether slimmers were male or female, fairly slim or very overweight, or whatever. A straight average calculated the following inch losses:

|  | *inches lost* | *(cm lost)* |
|---|---|---|
| Bust/chest | 1½ | (4) |
| Waist | 2½ | (6) |
| Hips | 2½ | (6) |
| Widest part | 2½ | (6) |
| Thighs (each) | 2 | (5) |
| Knees (each) | 1 | (2.5) |

The average weight loss was 2 lbs (1 kg) a week and the average length of time that this sample of slimmers had followed the diet was eight weeks.

I thought this was an amazing result, particularly because some of those following the diet admitted to being only fairly strict, whilst others only wanted to lose a few inches and very little weight. Any doctor would say that the ideal rate of weight loss is 1–2 lbs (0.5–1.0 kg) a week. This had worked out perfectly! However, as you will see in a later chapter, the best results were enjoyed by those who followed the diet very strictly.

Several of my very early correspondents continued to write and kept me posted of their progress. For instance Jo Higham, whose first letter I quoted in Chapter 1, wrote to me again in May. She said.

'I started your diet in late January weighing 10 st 5 lbs (66 kg); I am now 8 st 2 lbs (51.8 kg). I always was energetic but now I have even more energy than ever. I have totally changed my way of eating and the weight has dropped off – all from my rear and thighs! My ambition was to wear trousers, and this I can now do: I can wear size 10.

I did tell you in my first letter that my widest

part was *wide* – 44½ ins (113 cm), but my waist was only 26 ins (66 cm). The rest of me slim. All the diets never took it away.

Now my measurements are:

| | | | | | | |
|---|---|---|---|---|---|---|
| Widest part | 39 | ins | was 44½ ins | (99 was 113 cm) |
| Hips | 37 | ins | was 40 ins | (94 was 101 cm) |
| Waist | 24 | ins | was 26 ins | (61 was 66 cm) |
| Thighs | 22½ ins | was 25½ ins | (57 was 65 cm) |

I am so delighted and more so when my slim young daughter has asked to wear my new holiday things for her holiday in Barbados!

My husband and sisters can't believe it – I am so slim but so well. I eat like a horse, but healthier foods.

I used to eat buttered chips! But now I wouldn't dream of eating butter or margarine. Chocolates were like a drug – I've had one square since January and they no longer hold any appeal for me. I feel at 51 years a new woman, so much fitter and bursting with energy.'

You can, I am sure, appreciate my sheer delight at receiving such a happy, heart-warming letter from Jo; and I felt that Mrs K. B. said about herself exactly what many would be thinking this year:

'I shall continue the diet in the hope of displaying my thighs on the beach this summer without embarrassment for the first time!'

Finally, Mary Coppins-Brown wrote:

'It is a joy and pleasure to be able to wear straight dresses without any hip and thigh bulges, and to use the last hole instead of the first hole on belts! Thank you for allowing me to share in your successful diet.'

On the following pages I give details of the actual weight and inch losses enjoyed by just a sample of those who completed my questionnaire. I have indicated the age group in each case. Names have been stated where permission has been granted. The tables show the inch losses achieved and the resulting bust measurements, and clearly show that if you have a small bust you do not lose a great deal from it on this diet.

Not everyone lost a lot of weight and some lost more inches than weight. For instance Kathleen Frake only lost 3 lbs (1.4 kg) but she lost 1 in (2.5 cm) from her bust, 4½ ins (11 cm) from her waist, 4 ins (10 cm) from her hips and 1½ ins (4 cm) from each thigh! In fact I often advise people not to be too concerned with the scales – but do take the time and trouble to measure yourself. With this in mind you will notice that I have included Measurement Record Charts at the beginning of the book (pages 13–16).

|  |  |  |  | Inches lost from: | | |
| --- | --- | --- | --- | --- | --- | --- |
| Name | Age group | Weeks on diet | Weight lost lbs (kg) | Bust (cm) | Waist (cm) | Hips (cm) |
| Veronica Jarvis | 45–54 | 8 | 11 lbs (5 kg) | 3 (8 cm) | 3½ (9 cm) | 3 (8 cm) |
| Jill Davies | 35–44 | 6 | 10 lbs (4.5 kg) | 0 (0) | 2½ (6 cm) | 6 (15 cm) |
| Ruth Pike | 45–54 | 10 | 21 lbs (9.5 kg) | ½ (1 cm) | 3 (8 cm) | 4 (10 cm) |
| Susan Davies | 25–34 | 8 | 24 lbs (10.9 kg) | 2 (5 cm) | 3½ (9 cm) | 4 (10 cm) |
| Janet Lawrence | 45–54 | 8 | 17 lbs (7.7 kg) | 1 (2.5 cm) | 1¼ (3 cm) | 3 (8 cm) |
| Mrs B. B. | 45–54 | 8 | 17 lbs (7.7 kg) | 2 (5 cm) | 2½ (6 cm) | 2½ (6 cm) |
| Mrs. V. E. | 35–44 | 6 | 20 lbs (9.1 kg) | 0 (0) | 2 (5 cm) | 3 (8 cm) |
| Janet Lea | 35–44 | 8 | 17 lbs (7.7 kg) | 2 (5 cm) | 4 (10 cm) | 4 (10 cm) |
| Maxine Mansfield | 23 | 16 | 27 lbs (12.3 kg) | 1 (2.5 cm) | 4 (10 cm) | 4 (10 cm) |

| Inches lost from: | | | | | Bust measurement at end of diet ins (cm) | Height ft/ins (m) | Weight now st/lbs (kg) |
|---|---|---|---|---|---|---|---|
| Widest part (cm) | Thighs L. (cm) | R. (cm) | Knees L. (cm) | R. (cm) | | | |
| 3 (8 cm) | 2 (5 cm) | 2¼ (6 cm) | 1¼ (3 cm) | 1¼ (3 cm) | 37½ ins (95 cm) | 5 ft 8 ins (1.73 m) | 10 st 12 lbs (69.1 kg) |
| 5 (12.5 cm) | 4½ (11 cm) | 4½ (11 cm) | 3 (8 cm) | 3 (8 cm) | 34 ins (86 cm) | 5 ft 5½ ins (1.66 m) | 10 st 4 lbs (65.4 kg) |
| 3 (8 cm) | 2 (5 cm) | 2 (5 cm) | ½ (1 cm) | ½ (1 cm) | 34 ins (86 cm) | 5 ft 3 ins (1.60 m) | 9 st 7 lbs (60.4 kg) |
| 4½ (11 cm) | 2 (5 cm) | 1½ (4 cm) | 1 (2.5 cm) | 1½ (4 cm) | 39 ins (99 cm) | 5 ft 2 ins (1.58 m) | 11 st 6 lbs (72.7 kg) |
| 3 (8 cm) | 3½ (9 cm) | 3½ (9 cm) | 1½ (4 cm) | 1½ (4 cm) | 33½ ins (85 cm) | 5 ft 2 ins (1.58 m) | 9 st 6 lbs (60 kg) |
| 2½ (6 cm) | 3 (8 cm) | 3 (8 cm) | – | – | 34 ins (86 cm) | 5 ft 4 ins (1.63 m) | 9 st 0 lbs (57.1 kg) |
| – | 3 (8 cm) | 3 (8 cm) | – | – | 35 ins (89 cm) | 5 ft 5 ins (1.65 m) | 8 st 10 lbs (55.4 kg) |
| 3½ (9 cm) | 2½ (6 cm) | 2½ (6 cm) | ½ (1 cm) | – | 35 ins (89 cm) | 5 ft 4 ins (1.63 m) | 8 st 5 lbs (53.2 kg) |
| 5 (12.7 cm) | 3 (8 cm) | 3 (8 cm) | 2 (5 cm) | 2 (5 cm) | 34 ins (86 cm) | 5 ft 6 ins (1.68 m) | 8 st 6 lbs (53.6 kg) |

| Name | Age group | Weeks on diet | Weight lost lbs (kg) | Bust (cm) | Waist (cm) | Hips (cm) |
|---|---|---|---|---|---|---|
| | | | | *Inches lost from:* | | |
| Jeanne Dennett | 45–54 | 8 | 8 lbs (3.6 kg) | 0 (0) | 3 (8 cm) | 2¾ (7 cm) |
| Miss J. W. | 35–44 | 10 | 28 lbs (12.7 kg) | 1 (2.5 cm) | 3½ (9 cm) | 2¼ (6 cm) |
| Mrs A. C. | 45–54 | 10 | 23 lbs (10.5 kg) | 2 (5 cm) | 5 (12.5 cm) | 4 (10 cm) |
| Mrs A. Burton | 35–44 | 7 | 11 lbs (5 kg) | ½ (1 cm) | 2¼ (6 cm) | 2½ (6 cm) |
| Mrs. R. P. | 45–54 | 8 | 35 lbs (15.9 kg) | 2 (5 cm) | 4 (10 cm) | 4 (10 cm) |
| Mrs J. W. | 35–44 | 6 | 12 lbs (5.4 kg) | 3 (8 cm) | 2½ (6 cm) | 3 (8 cm) |
| Jackie Hadley | 25–34 | 17 | 31 lbs (14.1 kg) | 4 (10 cm) | 4½ (11 cm) | 4½ (11 cm) |
| Mrs S. W. | 45–54 | 14 | 28 lbs (12.7 kg) | 1½ (4 cm) | 4 (10 cm) | 11 (28 cm) |
| Meinir Jerman | 45–54 | 8 | 10 lbs (4.5 kg) | 1 (2.5 cm) | 2½ (6 cm) | 3½ (9 cm) |

| *Inches lost from:* | | | | | Bust | | |
|---|---|---|---|---|---|---|---|
| *Widest part* (cm) | *Thighs* L. (cm) | R. (cm) | *Knees* L. (cm) | R. (cm) | *measurement at end of diet* ins (cm) | *Height* ft/ins (m) | *Weight now* st/lbs (kg) |
| 3¾ (9.5 cm) | 3 (8 cm) | 3 (8 cm) | 2 (5 cm) | 2 (5 cm) | 34 ins (86 cm) | 5 ft 1 in (1.55 m) | 9 st 0 lbs (57.1 kg) |
| 2 (5 cm) | 2 (5 cm) | 2¾ (7 cm) | – | – | 36 ins (91 cm) | 5 ft 7 ins (1.70 m) | 10 st 11 lbs (68.6 kg) |
| 5 (12.7 cm) | 4 (10 cm) | 4 (10 cm) | 1 (2.5 cm) | 1 (2.5 cm) | 36 ins (91 cm) | 5 ft 5 ins (1.65 m) | 11 st 7 lbs (73.2 kg) |
| 2½ (6 cm) | 2½ (6 cm) | 2½ (6 cm) | ½ (1 cm) | ½ (1 cm) | 33½ ins (85 cm) | 5 ft 3 ins (1.60 m) | 8 st 0 lbs (50.9 kg) |
| 6 (15 cm) | 3 (8 cm) | 3 (8 cm) | 1½ (4 cm) | 1½ (4 cm) | 34 ins (86 cm) | 5 ft 2 ins (1.58 m) | 9 st 0¾ lbs (57.5 kg) |
| 2½ (6 cm) | 2½ (6 cm) | 3 (8 cm) | ½ (1 cm) | ½ (1 cm) | 40 ins (102 cm) | 5 ft 7½ ins (1.71 m) | 11 st 5 lbs (72.3 kg) |
| – | 3¾ (9.5 cm) | 3¾ (9.5 cm) | 2 (5 cm) | 1¾ (4 cm) | 32½ ins (83 cm) | 5 ft ½ in (1.53 m) | 7 st 11 lbs (49.5 kg) |
| 6½ (17 cm) | 5 (12.7 cm) | 5½ (14 cm) | 4 (10 cm) | 4¼ (11 cm) | 38 ins (97 cm) | 5 ft 6 ins (1.68 m) | 13 st 0 lbs (82.7 kg) |
| 2¼ (6 cm) | 3½ (9 cm) | 3 (8 cm) | 1 (2.5 cm) | ½ (1 cm) | 39 ins (99 cm) | 5 ft 5½ ins (1.66 m) | 11 st 0 lbs (70 kg) |

| Name | Age group | Weeks on diet | Weight lost lbs (kg) | Inches lost from: Bust (cm) | Waist (cm) | Hips (cm) |
|---|---|---|---|---|---|---|
| Elizabeth Mill | 55–64 | 10 | 20 lbs (9.1 kg) | 3½ (9 cm) | 6 (15 cm) | 4 (10 cm) |
| Pauline Perry | 35–44 | 8 | 19 lbs (8.6 kg) | 4 (10 cm) | 5 (12.7 cm) | 5 (12.7 cm) |
| Mrs D. Taylor | 45–54 | 9 | 18 lbs (8.2 kg) | 1 (2.5 cm) | 3 (8 cm) | 2½ (6 cm) |
| Alma Carwithen | 55–64 | 9 | 15 lbs (6.8 kg) | 3 (8 cm) | 2 (5 cm) | 3 (8 cm) |
| Avril Daley | 55–64 | 10 | 14 lbs (6.4 kg) | 3 (8 cm) | 3 (8 cm) | 2 (5 cm) |
| Doris Langley | 65–74 | 8 | 22 lbs (10 kg) | 4 (10 cm) | 3 (8 cm) | 4 (10 cm) |
| Angela Round | 35–44 | 11 | 11 lbs (5 kg) | ½ (1 cm) | 2½ (6 cm) | 3½ (9 cm) |
| Jeanne Ford | 45–54 | 7 | 14 lbs (6.4 kg) | 4 (10 cm) | 4½ (11 cm) | 4½ (11 cm) |
| Barbara Jones | 35–44 | 8 | 24 lbs (10.9 kg) | 3 (8 cm) | 3 (8 cm) | 4 (10 cm) |

| ches lost from: | | | | | Bust | | |
|---|---|---|---|---|---|---|---|
| idest rt m) | Thighs L. (cm) | R. (cm) | Knees L. (cm) | R. (cm) | measurement at end of diet ins (cm) | Height ft/ins (m) | Weight now st/lbs (kg) |
| cm) | 2 (5 cm) | 3 (8 cm) | 1½ (3.5 cm) | 1½ (3.5 cm) | 37 ins (94 cm) | 5 ft 6 ins (1.68 m) | 11 st 3 lbs (71.4 kg) |
| 0 cm) | 2 (5 cm) | 1 (2.5 cm) | 3½ (9 cm) | 2½ (6 cm) | 36 ins (91 cm) | 5 ft 6 ins (1.68 m) | 11 st 0 lbs (70 kg) |
| 0 cm) | 3 (8 cm) | 2½ (6 cm) | 2 (5 cm) | 1½ (3.5 cm) | 34 ins (86 cm) | 5 ft 5 ins (1.65 m) | 9 st 0 lbs (57.1 kg) |
| | 3 (8 cm) | 3 (8 cm) | — | — | 39 ins (99 cm) | 4 ft 11 ins (1.50 m) | 9 st 7 lbs (60.4 kg) |
| 5 cm) | 2½ (6 cm) | 1½ (4 cm) | 1 (2.5 cm) | 1 (2.5 cm) | 39 ins (99 cm) | 5 ft 5 ins (1.65 m) | 11 st 2 lbs (70.9 kg) |
| 0 cm) | 2 (5 cm) | 2½ (6 cm) | 1½ (4 cm) | 1 (2.5 cm) | 36 ins (91 cm) | 5 ft 4 ins (1.63 m) | 9 st 8 lbs (60.9 kg) |
| ½ cm) | 2½ (6 cm) | 2¾ (7 cm) | 1 (2.5 cm) | 1 (2.5 cm) | 37 ins (94 cm) | 5 ft 5½ ins (1.66 m) | 9 st 3 lbs (58.6 kg) |
| ½ cm) | 1¼ (3 cm) | 1¼ (3 cm) | 1⅛ (3 cm) | 1¼ (3 cm) | 36 ins (91 cm) | 5 ft 4 ins (1.63 cm) | 10 st 7 lbs (66.8 kg) |
| 0 cm) | 2½ (6 cm) | 2½ (6 cm) | 2 (5 cm) | 1½ (4 cm) | 38 ins (96 cm) | 5 ft 7 ins (1.70 m) | 11 st 0 lbs (70 kg) |

|                 |              |                   |                    | *Inches lost from:* |              |              |
|-----------------|--------------|-------------------|--------------------|---------------------|--------------|--------------|
| Name            | Age group    | Weeks on diet     | Weight lost lbs (kg) | Bust (cm)         | Waist (cm)   | Hips (cm)    |
| Janet Farrar    | 35–44        | 9                 | 22 lbs (10 kg)     | 2½ (6 cm)           | 2½ (6 cm)    | 4 (10 cm)    |
| Kathleen Frake  | 45–54        | 8                 | 3 lbs (1.4 kg)     | 1 (2.5 cm)          | 4½ (11 cm)   | 4 (10 cm)    |
| Pamela Smith    | 25–34        | 8                 | 24 lbs (10.9 kg)   | 3 (8 cm)            | 3½ (9 cm)    | 4¾ (12 cm)   |
| Maureen Watkins | 55–64        | 8                 | 18 lbs (8.2 kg)    | 3 (8 cm)            | 4 (10 cm)    | 2½ (6 cm)    |
| Nancy Watson    | 65–74        | 9                 | 16 lbs (7.3 kg)    | 2½ (6 cm)           | 4 (10 cm)    | 2½ (6 cm)    |
| Rachel Barnacle | 25–34        | 8                 | 7 lbs (3.2 kg)     | ½ (1 cm)            | 1 (2.5 cm)   | 1¾ (4 cm)    |
| Edward Bean     | 55–64        | 10                | 24 lbs (10.9 kg)   | 4 (10 cm)           | 5 (12.7 cm)  | 6 (15 cm)    |
| Gill Muir       | 25–34        | 8                 | 14 lbs (6.4 kg)    | 1½ (4 cm)           | 2 (2.5 cm)   | 3 (8 cm)     |
| Catherine Pike  | 15–24        | 18                | 42 lbs (19.1 kg)   | 3 (7.5 cm)          | 4½ (11 cm)   | 4½ (11 cm)   |

| Inches lost from: | | | | | Bust measurement at end of diet ins (cm) | Height ft/ins (m) | Weight now st/lbs (kg) |
| --- | --- | --- | --- | --- | --- | --- | --- |
| Widest part (cm) | Thighs L. (cm) | R. (cm) | Knees L. (cm) | R. (cm) | | | |
| 3½ (9 cm) | 2¾ (7 cm) | 3 (8 cm) | ¾ (2 cm) | 1½ (4 cm) | 36½ ins (92 cm) | 5 ft 3½ ins (1.61 m) | 10 st 1½ lbs (64.3 kg) |
| 2 (5 cm) | 1½ (4 cm) | 1½ (4 cm) | 1 (2.5 cm) | 1 (2.5 cm) | 35 ins (89 cm) | 5 ft 4 ins (1.63 m) | 9 st 0 lbs (57.1 kg) |
| 7 (18 cm) | 4½ (11 cm) | 4¾ (12 cm) | 3¼ (8 cm) | 3¾ (9 cm) | 34 ins (86 cm) | 5 ft 5½ ins (1.66 m) | 9 st 10 lbs (61.8 kg) |
| 3½ (9 cm) | 2 (5 cm) | 1½ (4 cm) | ¾ (2 cm) | ¾ (2 cm) | 36 ins (91 cm) | 5 ft 2½ ins (1.59 m) | 9 st 3 lbs (58.6 kg) |
| 3 (8 cm) | 2 (5 cm) | 1½ (4 cm) | 1 (2.5 cm) | 1 (2.5 cm) | 38 ins (96 cm) | 5 ft 6½ ins (1.69 m) | 11 st 2 lbs (70.9 kg) |
| 3¼ (8 cm) | 3 (8 cm) | 3¼ (8 cm) | 1½ (4 cm) | 1½ (4 cm) | 32 ins (81 cm) | 5 ft 6 ins (1.68 m) | 8 st 2 lbs (51.8 kg) |
| 6 (15 cm) | 3 (8 cm) | 3 (8 cm) | 1½ (4 cm) | 1½ (4 cm) | 42 ins (107 cm) | 6 ft 4 ins (1.93 m) | 15 st 10 lbs (100 kg) |
| 3½ (9 cm) | 2 (5 cm) | 2 (5 cm) | 1½ (4 cm) | 1½ (4 cm) | 33½ ins (85 cm) | 5 ft 5 ins (1.65 m) | 9 st 0 lbs (57.1 kg) |
| 6 (15 cm) | 5 (12.7 cm) | 5 (12.7 cm) | 2 (5 cm) | 2 (5 cm) | 37 ins (94 cm) | 5 ft 9 ins (1.75 m) | 11 st 2 lbs (70.9 kg) |

# 4
# The 'Tum and Bum Diet' for men

Some weeks after the diet had been published I spoke to the Associate Editor of the *Sunday Express*. He said, 'I've been following the diet since you gave me a copy and I've lost 13 lbs (5.9 kg) and have lost inches exactly from where I wanted – just around my middle. In fact we men have renamed it the "Tum and Bum Diet".' Men do not have to worry about jodhpur thighs as that isn't normally where they put on excess weight – it is almost always around the middle. Whilst women have 'thunder thighs' or 'child-bearing hips' men suffer from a 'beer belly'.

On my previous trials only three men had participated, but this time I had lots of husband-and-wife teams who wrote to me quite spontaneously about their successes. In my replies (I replied to everybody who wrote to me) I asked if they would be kind enough to complete a questionnaire. The results were wonderful. Here are just a few.

Evelyn Eaglestone wrote telling me how she and her husband both felt the diet was ideal for them, 'We just cannot believe that we can tuck into such lovely food and still lose weight.' Evelyn's husband,

Stanley, lost 15 lbs (6.8 kg) in eight weeks and lost 4 ins (10 cm) from around his waist (he only took this measurement). Evelyn lost an amazing 21 lbs (9.5 kg), losing 1 inch (2.5 cm) from her bust, 2 ins (5 cm) from her waist, 3 ins (7.5 cm) from both her hips and widest part and 2 ins (5 cm) from her thighs. She said, 'Other diets have left me feeling so low and hungry that I've said "Life is too short to suffer this", and that "I would rather die of overeating than starvation," but with your diet you've got the best of both worlds. Eat plenty *and* lose weight! What more could anyone wish for?' She continued:

'I must tell you what really made me realize I was so overweight. All winter I went round the house in a bright green track-suit (extra large). One day I opened the door to the milkman. "You look smart in your green," he said. "Yes" I said, "kidding myself I'm the green goddess!" "Well," said he, "I was thinking more of the Jolly Green Giant!" We both rolled up laughing but it made me think.'

Mrs J. B. explained that her husband suffered from high blood pressure and joined her on the diet. 'He lost 17½ lbs (8 kg) and felt better for it.' She also explained that she had lost weight a couple of times before with the help of a slimming club but whilst she might have lost more weight on these occasions it didn't seem to go from the areas she *wanted* to slim. Family and friends always commented on the fact that her face looked drawn, but not this time. 'In fact my sister asked me which diet I'd been following and went out immediately and bought your book.'

One married couple who wished to remain anonymous wrote:

'We must say this is the first time that we have stayed on any diet as long as this without great hardship – we both have 1 stone (6.4 kg) to lose and hope to make it.'

After eight weeks the husband had lost 12 lbs (5.4 kg) whilst his wife had lost 9 lbs (4.1 kg).

I was particularly pleased to receive a letter from a vicar's wife and to hear that she and her husband had been following my diet. (Being a committed Christian myself, I am always particularly delighted to hear from anyone connected with the Church. In fact, I hold a slimming and exercise class at home for a few of my friends from my local church and I have never had the pleasure of taking such a lovely, happy, noisy exercise class and one where the weight losses are so consistently good.) Here is what Mrs K., the vicar's wife, said:

'I feel I must write to you about the success we have had on your diet. Both my husband and I started it the week that the article appeared in the *Sunday Express*. As soon as the book was published we were able to get down to it properly. We have both literally changed shape!
I have lost 12 lbs (5.4 kg), nearly all of it from my hips, 47 ins (119 cm) down to 41 ins (104 cm), and 2 ins (5 cm) from my waist. My

husband is 1¼ st (8 kg) lighter and has to wear braces to keep his trousers from falling down.

The best thing about this diet apart from losing weight in the right places, is that there is no calorie counting as such. Wherever we are we can avoid, or restrict, one type of food, and most of the time it is not apparent that we *are* dieting. I call it the *quiet diet!*

Now that we have lost weight so noticeably people are showing interest and I have no doubt that there will be a lot of fat lost in this county this summer.'

Mrs K. lost 1 in (2.5 cm) from her bust, making it 36 ins (91 cm), 2 ins (5 cm) from her waist and 6 ins (15 cm) from her hips. After eight weeks Mrs K. had lost 15 lbs (6.8 kg) whilst the Reverend K. had lost 21 lbs (9.5 kg).

On the subject of the *quiet diet* one lady wrote:

'Amazingly successful. I have a husband who is a big eater and any diet I attempted was a failure since he thought I was starving. This diet I can follow without him even noticing I'm on one.

I lost 7 lbs (3.2 kg) within the first ten days and then nothing for a week, but have lost steadily but slowly since. I must modify the diet for the next ten days as we have guests and are going away, but I shall be able to cut out almost all fats without anyone being the wiser. I feel marvellous, am able to bend and walk briskly, and the arthritis in my knees is greatly improved. Having achieved my objective to lose a stone

(6.4 kg) by Easter, I am now aiming for a weight of 11 st (70 kg), and ultimately 10 st 7 lbs (66.8 kg). I am so grateful to you – the weight loss is gratifying but even better is the loss of inches and the emerging of hips and waist.

I passed your diet on to two friends who didn't quite believe me; they have each lost 8 lbs (3.6 kg) and have happily eaten their words.'

Mrs Beatrice Love wrote that her husband had topped 14 st (89 kg) after Christmas. At 5ft 8ins (1.73 m) and working as a painter and decorator, Mrs Love explained that 'he felt far from well, bloated and uncomfortable. Nothing fitted him and his weight was hampering his climbing and bending.' She continued:

'We both began to follow your diet the day after reading the *Sunday Express* and as soon as your book appeared in the shops I bought it. We've never looked back from then. Bill wants to lose another 5 lbs (2.3 kg) or so, bringing him to 11½ st (73.2 kg), he's now 11 st 12 lbs (75.4 kg). He's regaining his boyish figure. My weight had shot up to 10 st 10 lbs (68.2 kg), I'm 5 ft 4 ins (1.62 m). I'm now 9½ st (60.4 kg) and would like to lose another stone (6.4 kg). I'm thrilled about how the fat has gone from my thighs, waist and hips, and my figure is showing some resemblance to the way it looked in my twenties. In fact we are both feeling younger and healthier and our way of life now will be a fat-free one.'

Veronica Jarvis started the diet on her own but after a fortnight her husband joined her.

'I found it much easier, and even visitors have been surprised how well we eat and have joined the Hip and Thigh Brigade. Thanks a million, Rosemary.

P.S. It's not like being on a diet. We were amazed how easy it was to adapt to.'

Ken Wilkins was one of the few men who actually completed the comments section of the questionnaire himself. He wrote:

'I read your book which my wife had bought. She started the diet, so as moral support I followed her eating routine with her. I thought I wasn't overweight at 11 st 2 lbs (70.9 kg). I was amazed at the loss of weight to 10 st 7 lbs (66.8 kg) and not any ill effects yet! Your book contains good sense for a healthy body.'

Mr Edward Bean wrote:

'I feel I can recommend this diet to anybody. My introduction to the Hip and Thigh Diet came by way of a visit to a friend in London. He had a wife who I always knew as a rotund person. Imagine my astonishment when I saw her after a long parting as a very slim youthful figure. My mind was immediately made up and I started there and then.'

Margaret and Douglas Hirst wrote:

'After hearing and reading such glowing reports of your Hip and Thigh Diet I decided it was exactly what was needed by my husband and I. That was six weeks ago. My husband is now 1 st (6.4 kg) lighter – 15 st to 14 (95 kg to 89 kg), all off the offending bulge in front. I have lost ½ st (3.2 kg) – from 9½ to 9 st (60.5 kg to 57 kg). We thoroughly enjoy your menus and eat them heartily, never feeling hungry between meals – though we still occasionally long for a chocolate.'

In their questionnaire which they completed after writing to me, Mrs Hirst explained that she didn't really need to diet 'though I am thrilled that I have lost my spare tyre!' She only followed the diet because her husband needed to lose weight and it made life easier if they both ate the same meals.

'The meals are so enjoyable and appetizing. I prefer them to the meals we used to eat.'

Mr Hirst explained that he had had heart surgery so a very low fat diet was ideal for his condition.

'I feel 100% better since I started the diet. You see I used to eat a large packet of Rennies per month. Since starting the diet I haven't eaten one. You have my permission to quote me if you wish. Perhaps the manufacturers of Rennies won't be pleased, but so be it!'

Mr R. E. lost all his excess weight in eight weeks – a remarkable 21 lbs (9.5 kg). He lost 2½ ins (6 cm) from his chest, 2 ins (5 cm) from his waist and 2½ ins (6 cm) from his hips. Mrs E. lost less weight by comparison, but is quite small boned taking very small-sized shoes and measuring only 4ft 10 ins (1.47 m) tall. In eleven weeks she reduced her weight by 14 lbs (6.4 kg) to 8 st 2 lbs (51.8 kg). She was amazed at the 4½ ins (11 cm) lost from her hips and over 2 ins (5 cm) from each thigh and commented on how much her tummy had reduced. I had to smile when she wrote:

'My husband tells me that since being on the diet I have stopped snoring – he is delighted!'

# 5
# Eat your way to better health

When a smoker dies of lung cancer, the poor victim is almost always blamed for his or her own death. 'It's not surprising she met an early grave, she's smoked forty a day ever since I've known her and that's thirty years,' and, 'What do you expect, smoking all her life – God rest her soul,' are common judgements made by those left behind.

Among many other factors, it is probably true that smoking may be a contributory cause of the disease. But the point is that lung cancer is *immediately* connected with smoking, in everybody's mind.

On the other hand, if someone dies of a heart attack it is just accepted that the cause is hereditary, 'He over-exerted himself once too often,' or most commonly, it was 'Just bad luck'. We have not yet been sufficiently educated to realize that the risk of dying from the greatest killer disease in the Western world could be drastically reduced if only we took preventative measures by eating sensibly and looking after our bodies. The earlier we take these steps the better for everyone concerned.

One in four deaths in this country is caused by heart disease. This year over 200,000 people will die from heart disease; that's Wembley stadium filled to capacity twice over! No other condition claims so many lives – yet how many people really know what risks they run? If you were to ask twenty men or women in the street what they should do to avoid heart disease the majority would say, 'take more exercise, and eat margarine instead of butter.' We are, in reality, extremely ignorant of the various causes of this greatest killer disease.

Whilst there are many types of heart disease, the most common and the most tragic is the type that causes heart attacks and is called coronary heart disease. Here's how it comes about:

Most of us have seen a heart in one form or another, whether on television or in school or even at the butchers. The human heart is about the size of a fist and is a muscle filled with blood. It contracts about seventy times a minute pumping blood around our body. The heart needs a constant good supply of oxygen which it gets from the bloodstream. However, the heart's own oxygen supply is not taken from the blood which is continually being pumped through it to service the rest of the body, but from separate little arteries which are called coronary arteries. These branch off from the main artery, called the aorta, and then divide into lots of smaller branches which are all over the surface of the heart.

The problems start in early adult life when the walls of these coronary arteries become 'furred up' and narrower. The narrowing is caused by a fatty deposit called atheroma and if it gets too thick and the coronary arteries too narrow, the blood supply to the heart becomes restricted or even blocked. This condition is called 'coronary heart disease'.

The disease has two main forms, angina and

heart attack. Angina occurs when the coronary arteries have become narrower very gradually and is only noticed when the heart has to work harder than usual. The symptoms of angina are a heavy cramp-like pain across the chest which can spread to the neck, shoulder, arm and even the jaw. Angina is quite different from a heart attack because it is usually relieved by a short period of rest or relaxation. It can also be relieved or controlled by drugs and in severe cases, surgery.

On the other hand, a heart attack occurs when there is a sudden and severe blockage in one of the coronary arteries so that the blood supply to part of the heart is actually cut off. The blockage is usually caused by a blood clot forming in an artery already narrowed by fatty atheroma. This is called a coronary thrombosis or just 'a coronary'. In some cases the effects of the blockage can be so severe that the heart stops beating altogether and this is called a cardiac arrest. Unless the heart starts beating again within a few minutes the person will die, and in 50% of all fatal heart attacks the victim dies within thirty minutes.

The pain is a crushing vice-like ache felt in the chest. It can also spread to the neck, arm or jaw and doesn't usually ease off for several hours. Sickness, giddiness and feelings of faintness often accompany the pain.

There are many factors which affect our vulnerability to heart disease. As well as our family history, sex and age, we must also consider how physically active we are, the amount of stress we have to endure, whether or not we smoke, what we eat and, very importantly, whether or not we are overweight.

People who have a family history of heart disease are undoubtedly at greater risk. It is obvious that they should take *particular* care to follow preventative guidelines to reduce their risk to a minimum. There is no doubt that the older we get the greater is the risk of suffering a heart attack. The narrowing of the arteries which can lead to angina and heart attacks tends to increase with age. Men are more at risk from heart disease than women. In fact a man in his late forties is five times more likely to die of heart disease than a woman of the same age. But it would be a mistake for women to consider themselves reasonably 'safe', because after the menopause a woman loses the protective effect of her hormones and her chances of suffering from heart disease are almost equal to a man's. In recent years there has in fact been an increased incidence of heart disease in women in their thirties and forties.

Apart from age, sex and family history, the other contributory factors are voluntary so the choice really is ours!

Cigarette smoking can double our risk of dying from a heart attack and heavy smokers are even more likely to die young. For instance a man who is over fifty and who smokes over twenty cigarettes a day is *four* times more likely to suffer from heart disease than a non-smoker of the same age. Women smokers are at just as much risk as men and at even greater risk if over the age of thirty-five and on the pill. The answer here must be to give up smoking – as soon as you do, you begin to reduce the risk of a heart attack. And the good news is that you could be almost back to a non-smoker's risk level within a few years. Cutting down or smoking low tar cigarettes will not protect you against heart disease.

The reason cigarette smoking adversely affects the heart is because the nicotine in tobacco smoke increases the blood pressure. This is because the carbon monoxide content of cigarette smoke cuts down the amount of oxygen in the blood and accordingly the heart has to work harder yet it is getting less oxygen. Smoking also speeds up the 'furring up' of the arteries in the heart. Smoking is bad news from every direction – from being damaging to your health and the health of those around you to being smelly and totally antisocial.

A great deal of heart disease could also be prevented if everyone over the age of thirty-five had their blood pressure checked every few years by their doctor. Blood pressure is the pressure which the heart and arteries apply in order to squeeze the blood around the body. When we are sitting or resting our blood pressure remains at a steady resting level. This level increases depending on our activity and the demand for a surge of blood to be sent where it is needed, for instance to the muscles during exercise or to our brain when under pressure mentally. As soon as we stop exerting ourselves the blood pressure returns to normal again.

Hypertension, or high blood pressure, is when the resting blood pressure is higher than normal. Whilst high blood pressure is rare among young people it is common among those over thirty-five, no doubt caused by following an unhealthy lifestyle – eating too much, consuming too much alcohol, having too much salt in our food, smoking, lack of exercise, and suffering from too much stress. Unfortunately most people have no idea that they have high blood pressure because it doesn't actually *feel* any different. But high blood pressure makes the heart work harder resulting in heart disease. There is also the danger of a stroke which is when a blood clot occurs in the brain and the blood supply is cut off.

The good news is that blood pressure can be helped enormously by reducing your weight to its correct level, by not drinking too much alcohol, by stopping smoking, eating less salt, increasing the amount of exercise and by learning to relax.

Stress and anxiety are often self-inflicted. I believe that every problem can be resolved, and that if it can be approached sensibly and thoughtfully, it can even be turned to advantage. If ignored, stress not only contributes to physical disorders such as heart disease, high blood pressure, ulcers and asthma, it can also lead to a variety of mental illnesses of which insomnia, depression and irritability are just early symptoms. On the other hand, if we are under-stressed we will become lethargic and tired and psychosomatic illnesses could occur. A certain amount of stress, therefore, is an essential part of our everyday life. It keeps us on our toes.

Whilst exercise is regularly advocated as essential to a healthy heart this recommendation is often misunderstood. If an overweight man in his fifties who is a heavy smoker, has a family history of heart disease and is working in a stressful job were to decide to 'get fit' and invite a colleague for a game of squash for the first time in twenty years, he would be doing just about the best he could to give himself a heart attack. His heart just would not be able to cope with the strain. The heart will benefit most from the kind of exercise that builds up stamina – the ability to keep going without gasping for breath. Stamina depends on the efficiency of our muscles and circulation and of course the most important muscle of all is the heart itself.

Regular moderate exercise such as brisk walking is the answer for the gentleman described above. As he becomes fitter he may be able to do more and more, but moderation is the key factor. Playing golf or walking the dog is ideal exercise for anyone and the fresh air will be beneficial too. In order to build stamina something more energetic like swimming, cycling or keeping fit to music can be very beneficial and enjoyable. Regular exercise of this kind improves the balance of fatty substances in the blood stream, lowers the resting blood pressure level and strengthens the heart muscle. But whatever it is we decide to do, it must be continued in the long term. A mad spurt of extreme physical activity for two weeks a year will do us nothing but harm. It is therefore essential to find a form of activity we enjoy so that we are happy to practise it two or three times a week and continue it for life.

So now to the problem of obesity. Obesity can also increase the risk of heart disease, not in itself but because of the many other conditions it can create, conditions which most certainly *do* contribute to heart disease (high blood pressure and diabetes are the most common). The more overweight you are the more likely you are to get high blood pressure and diabetes. Often members of my slimming classes have been referred to me by their doctors, anxious for their patients to reduce their weight and so help reduce their blood pressure. As soon as they lose weight their blood pressure returns to normal.

Don't forget it is not just ourselves we are putting at risk. If we serve bad-for-you foods at home we affect our own hearts, certainly, but worse still, we are serving the wrong food to our families. We have their hearts in our hands too.

There is little doubt that to have become obese in the first instance we have simply eaten too much of the wrong sorts of foods. In other words, too many fatty and sugary foods which are positively loaded with calories – bread spread with lashings of butter, an abundance of fried foods, cream cakes, biscuits, chocolate, crisps and so on. The types of foods overweight people love.

The fat in our food is not only responsible for the extra inches on our hips. It can also push up our blood cholesterol level. (See page 72 for list of foods high in cholesterol.) Cholesterol is a natural substance in the blood and is mostly made from the fat in the food we eat, though the body itself is quite capable of making an adequate supply. If there is a lot of fat in our diet we have a high cholesterol level. This can have the effect of accelerating the build-up of atheroma which in turn eventually leads to heart disease. Therefore the higher the level of cholesterol in the blood the greater the risk of problems with the heart.

There has been so much talk of saturated and unsaturated fats that most people have heard of them. Few, however, actually understand what they are. The difference between the two types is their chemical make-up and whilst I don't want to go into lengthy explanations about the proportions of carbon and hydrogen atoms that determine the types of fatty acids it is important to realize that fat isn't just a single compound but comes in many forms. All fats are made up of fatty acids: some of these are saturated fatty acids (called saturates), the rest are unsaturated and these include a special group called polyunsaturated fatty acids (or polyunsaturates). Different fats have different proportions of various fatty acids. Most are high in saturates but some are high in polyunsaturates.

As far as the heart is concerned saturates are considered the main enemy. If we eat too much food high in saturates it can increase our blood cholesterol level and that in turn increases our risk of heart disease. Saturated fat is to be found mostly in animal products like cream, butter, eggs, offal, and in the fat on meat and poultry. In place of butter or margarine, alternatives such as Flora are recommended as it is high in polyunsaturates.

It would be a mistake to *increase* the consumption of foods high in polyunsaturates in the belief that they will 'do us good'. We must, after all, remember that we can produce sufficient cholesterol within our own bodies and that fats high in polyunsaturates contain the same amount of calories as the original saturated products so they do not aid slimming in any way.

So this now leaves us with the view that if we reduce our intake of *all* fat our health will certainly benefit and so will our waistlines. And whilst it is impossible to state categorically that heart disease can be caused by eating too much fat, in recent investigations it was observed that among the groups of people who consumed high amounts of fat the incidence of heart attack was far higher than among those who followed a low fat diet. It would be easy to conclude from this research that fat can actually cause heart disease but with so many other factors to be taken into consideration it is impossible to make such a simple statement. However, it *is* generally acknowledged that to reduce the consumption of fat in our daily diet will almost certainly reduce the risk of heart disease along with other medical conditions.

So how much fat do we actually need? The average consumption of fat in the Western world at the present time is about 130 grams (over 4½ ounces) a day per person. This fat includes everything from the obvious fats like butter and oil to those hidden in cakes, biscuits and fried foods. The amount of fat we actually *need* is staggeringly low at 5 grams (less than a quarter of an ounce) per day, providing it contains the right kind of fatty acids. As I do not suggest or recommend that we reduce our intake to such a very low level, we need not concern ourselves that we will eat insufficient quantities to endanger our health. However, it is clear that currently far too much fat is consumed and it is an ideal area in which to make a significant reduction without fear of nutrient deficiency.

So to sum up, if we want to help ourselves towards a healthy heart and a long and happy life we need to eat a low fat diet, take regular exercise and stop smoking. If we can reduce our weight to around that of our youth and eat well enough to give us the energy to work and live our lives to the full, we will all benefit. In addition, we will make our GPs very happy!

Many of my readers have written to tell me how much their health has benefited from following my low fat Hip and Thigh Diet. So, while I am not suggesting that my diet will cure or even help anyone suffering from a particular medical condition, I would like everyone to share the experiences of the many people who have found they feel more healthy, more active – much better in every way – since adopting a low fat diet. If you are suffering from any illness or medical condition, it is *always* better to go and see your doctor before you start a diet, to discuss how it will affect you.

Now let's see how readers suffering from different conditions have felt while following the diet:

## Arthritis

Audrey Bewley wrote:

'I suffer from osteoarthritis in my knees. The pain is much reduced and I can walk more easily through the weight loss. The most important comment I have to make is that the awful indigestion and heartburn have disappeared. I truly love the diet and intend keeping to a low fat diet for the rest of my life.'

Mrs Dennett wrote:

'The results are superb . . . my arthritis has diminished in my feet and hands. Thanks a million.'

One lady whose age fell into the 75–84 age group in the questionnaire told me that she had developed arthritis in her right leg last year, and had gained a lot of weight caused by the enforced immobility.

'I am now able to move about much more easily – thanks to you and your most excellent diet. I am amazed to find that I am never hungry whereas before I was always thinking about my next meal. I shall never return to my old way of eating!'

Another lady wrote:

'I feel marvellous, am able to bend and walk briskly and the arthritis in my knees is greatly improved.'

Mrs E. K. wrote:

'Amazed how quickly flesh fell away. In two months I lost 1½ st (9.5 kg) – this cannot be bad! Have tried calorie *control* and lost 5 lbs (2.3 kg) in a fortnight and then stuck.

The effect on health, too, has been astounding. Neck and upper arm arthritis gone and lower back vastly improved (having had spinal fusion, the most I can hope for.)

My whole outlook on life has vastly improved and I feel younger than my 73 years. I have regained that sparkle. Many thanks.'

Mrs S. W. lost 28 lbs (12.7 kg) in fourteen weeks and with it a staggering 11 ins (28 cm) from her hips! She lost only 1½ ins (4 cm) from her bust, 4 ins (10 cm) from her waist and 5 ins (12.7 cm) from each thigh.

'We have quite a history of rheumatism and arthritis in our family and before losing the weight on the diet I had several twinges in my hips. But with less weight to carry around I have had no more problems.'

Then I received a completed questionnaire from a doctor who had followed the diet and lost 12 lbs (5.4 kg) in seven weeks. This is what she wrote:

'I am actually a doctor interested in, though not dealing in or treating, nutritional problems. I am involved, voluntarily, in Arthritis Care and have recommended this diet to several of our members. Excess weight aggravates arthritis, and yet forced inactivity, because of disability, promotes weight gain.

It remains to be seen how our members benefit from this regime – certainly they cannot take others (the very low calorie branded powder products) as they can interfere with their drug treatments.

I intend to stick with the diet and lose more, but am satisfied with the steady loss.'

## Blood pressure

It is generally accepted that overweight and bad eating habits can contribute to high blood pressure and by reducing weight and amending our diet the problem can be helped greatly. These are some of the comments I received from readers of the Hip and Thigh Diet:

Mrs E. D. S. wrote:

'I am convinced that having red meat only

twice a week has reduced my blood pressure. The last count was the lowest for nine years.'

Mrs E. B., having lost 2 st (12.7 kg), wrote:

'My doctor is especially pleased as my high blood pressure has gone down five points.'

Mr and Mrs C. wrote to say how delighted they were that both their blood pressure and cholesterol levels had reduced. Mrs C. added:

'I have had high blood pressure since the start of my change of life, also asthma and hot flushes. My blood pressure has gone down from 140/90 to 130/85 since starting the diet; for my asthma I only need to take my spray 2–3 times a week; and as for my hot flushes, I am having a good night's sleep, which my husband is more than pleased about. My husband has lost 10 lbs (4.5 kg) and feels so much better and has a lot more energy.'

Mrs Muriel Wilce lost 12 lbs (5.4 kg) in eight weeks. She had suffered from high blood pressure and high cholesterol, so this diet was ideal for her.

'The Practice Nurse was delighted that I had lost so much weight when I recently went for a blood pressure check.'

# Cholesterol

## Notes to cholesterol patients
The low fat diet described in this book will certainly help those who suffer from high cholesterol, but some foods whilst low in fat are actually very high in cholesterol and anyone who has a high-cholesterol problem should avoid the following foods:

Eggs, egg dishes, Scotch eggs
Offal: Brain, heart, kidney, liver, sweetbread, tongue, liver sausage, pâté
Duck, dark meat of chicken or turkey, steak and kidney pie, lamb, pork, salami
Fish roe, kedgeree, taramasalata
Butter, margarine, cream, cheese, suet
Pastry, cakes, biscuits, buns
Seafood including crab, lobster, prawns, scampi, shrimps, mussels, whelks, winkles
Nuts including peanuts, cashews
Olives
Mayonnaise, salad cream
Chocolate, crisps
Coconut and coconut oil
Lemon curd

# Coelic disease

This is a digestive disorder requiring the patient to adhere strictly to a gluten-free diet.

Maureen Watkins reported the effects of the Hip and Thigh Diet on her shape, though of course there would have been many foods suggested in the diet that Maureen would have had to avoid.

'I am a coeliac on a gluten-free diet. Before being diagnosed two years ago my tummy was distended (one of the symptoms). On the gluten-free diet I put on weight and went up two dress sizes. The consultant told me I would put on weight and didn't hold out much hope of my tummy reducing.

Though the tummy is still more prominent than I like, there is much less of it and I can pull it in to look better.

I saw my consultant after four weeks on your diet, told him I was losing 2 lbs (0.9 kg) a week and he said it was fine to continue as eating less fat would be good for me.

I certainly feel and look much better. I have also noticed that my wrists and fingers have slimmed down.

I am continuing with the diet.'

## Constipation

Because the diet contains so much natural fibre in the form of fruit, vegetables, cereals and wholemeal bread, I felt confident that it would help many who suffered from constipation. I asked about this in my questionnaire and 82.2% said they experienced no problems with constipation whilst on the diet. Indeed, many said the diet had definitely helped them to become regular after a history of constipation.

## Gall stones

As I explained at the beginning of this book, it was due to my own gall stones that this diet was discovered. After my first book about the Hip and Thigh Diet was published I received many letters from fellow sufferers who had avoided surgery by following a very low fat diet and who, like me, had enjoyed the side effect of reduced inches on their hips and thighs.

Needless to say there were lots of people who were suffering with gall stones, and awaiting surgery, who were delighted when my Hip and Thigh Diet book was published. It gave them a 'handbook of how to avoid fat' – the very food that causes the gall bladder to work and to disturb your gall stones if you have the misfortune to have them.

Here are two extracts from the many letters I received from gall-stone sufferers. Mrs Brenchley wrote:

'I am a 62-year-old diabetic with several other health problems and have now had a rather large gall stone diagnosed. They are *very* reluctant to operate, although I have had very severe attacks during the last two years, (they only give me a 50–50 chance of success) and I have had to 'learn to live with it'. Your book has helped me to do just that. Since buying it, I have enjoyed the best health I've had for years, as I now know exactly what foods to avoid and am still able to keep up my quota of carbohydrates for the Insulin. I have begun to lose weight very slowly *but* steadily. I showed the book to my doctor at King's College Diabetic Clinic, telling her what I was doing – and she agreed that she has seen a great improvement in me. So, I for one, am a very satisfied customer.'

Mrs Joyce Williams wrote:

> 'I started following your diet as soon as I was able to obtain a copy of your book. My reason was to avoid surgery for gall stones – I am seeing a surgeon in three weeks' time – and so far the pain has gone, and so has the excess fat exactly where you said it would! I would like to know if you get any pain now and whether the stones disappear or pass through, or whether they lie quietly waiting for the next indiscretion with food.
>
> I am not looking forward to meeting the surgeon because I imagine he will not be pleased with me when I refuse any surgery offered.'

I replied explaining that fortunately I had not experienced any further discomfort since changing from a very high fat to a very low fat regime, despite the occasional 'indiscretion'. I sent Joyce a questionnaire, and when she replied whe wrote:

> 'My gall-stone problem has seemingly disappeared. The weight loss has been a bonus!
>
> I see the surgeon on 11 April and intend to show him your book and to tell him of my improvement. I only had one "bad" episode – nothing like yours – in November, and have waited until April for my appointment! If I elected to have an operation I suppose it could well be a few years before my turn came. I will never again budge from this diet.'

I hope Joyce's gall stones have continued to give her no more trouble but I must point out that an illness is never the same for any two people. I have no doubt that for many my low fat diet can help enormously in the relief of pain caused by gall stones. I would *never* suggest that you go against the advice of your doctor or surgeon; but there is, I believe, no harm in asking first to try all other avenues to avoid surgery. If this fails, at least you will feel satisfied that you've done what you can. If you *do* avoid surgery of course it could just help the hospital queues too!

## Heart disease

Heart disease is the biggest killer in the Western world. It can be caused by a combination of many factors. If it runs in the family, you are a male, you smoke, are overweight and have a stressful life, take very little exercise and eat a lot of fatty food – watch out! I don't wish to alarm you, but these are the facts; and we can do *so* much to help ourselves. Women are by no means free from risk, particularly after the menopause when the protective hormones diminish. Never has help been so available to those who are most at risk. The whole medical profession is keen to encourage prevention of heart disease which, for most, *is* avoidable. And it's never too late to start.

Mrs Marsh wrote to me about her husband who had decided to use my Hip and Thigh Diet to help stave off a likely heart attack:

'We used the book not just to lose weight but for medical reasons, my husband *had* to go on a fat- and cholesterol-free diet. He had been told that, with his family history and his high blood fat count, he would have a heart attack within five years – probably fatal. He is 43. We were given a diet sheet. Your book made things much easier.

He went for follow-up tests in February – three months after sticking very strictly to the diet.

His blood fat count is down by 30% and the doctor is very pleased and told him to stick to whatever he is doing, and wishes everyone would do the same. His chances of a fatal heart attack have been cut drastically.

The side effects are: we are all, two daughters and ourselves, on a very healthy diet and I have a lean, trim husband again. From us you deserve a *thank you*.'

On the questionnaire which Mrs Marsh completed on behalf of her husband, she added:

'The diet is a permanent feature of this household, but because of its excellent success rate, when we do have a meal out, we can relax a little and though we do not binge as such, the occasional "wrong" foods are acceptable. Where there has been weight loss we did not take measurements as that was not the *reason* for the diet, but a happy side effect.'

Douglas Hirst, another heart patient, wrote this on his questionnaire:

'I shall still carry on with this diet because I want to try and reach 13 st (82.7 kg). I have had heart surgery and this fat free diet is so good for my condition. I feel 100% better since I started it.'

## Hiatus hernia

An hiatus hernia is a most unpleasant condition which has the effect of allowing food that has been eaten to be regurgitated, and constant belching is experienced by sufferers.

Mrs K. Hayman wrote on her questionnaire:

'I have had quite a lot of trouble with an hiatus hernia for some years. Since going on this diet, I am so much better; no coughing or sickness and I have been able to cut down on the tablets I have to take after meals. It is a wonderful feeling to know I can go anywhere without coughing and worrying about other people.
I thought you would like to see the *dos* and *don'ts* of having an hiatus hernia, and how your diet helps so much.'

Mrs Hayman enclosed a useful list of *dos* and *don'ts* for hiatus hernia sufferers in the hope that they may help other people:

| *Dos* | *Don'ts* |
|---|---|
| Eat little and often (about 2-hourly). | Eat and drink at same meal. |
| All liquids including soup should be taken not less than 1 hour before or after solid food. | Eat more than 2 courses at any time. |
| | Drink anything that is too hot or ice cold. |

| | |
|---|---|
| Chew your food very thoroughly. | Drink normal tea or coffee as it creates acid. |
| Peel fruit and tomatoes as the skin is indigestible. | Take white sugar, white bread or white rice. |
| Drink fruit juices, herb tea, or China tea. | Bend forward when lifting or picking up anything, but bend the knees as you lift. |
| Sweeten with honey or natural brown sugar. | |
| Try to avoid coughing – it can enlarge the hernia. | Never stretch your arms upwards and avoid wearing restrictive clothing. |
| Try to sleep on high propped-up pillows at night. | |

Mrs B. R. followed my diet and wrote:

'Having suffered quite severely from an hiatus hernia since 1980 I find the need for less medication than for many years ... so nice to be free from the dreadful chest pain I had at times, bringing me to many tears.'

I received a lovely letter from May Tapp. With her permission I am quoting it all:

'I would like to say thank you for your book – *Hip and Thigh Diet*. I have followed it to the letter for nearly four months and have lost almost 2 st (12.7 kg) in weight, and all from the right places. The biggest bonus, however, is in how much better I feel. I have angina, an hiatus hernia and a few more problems. The hernia had got completely out of control and I was never free from pain, but almost from the first day of this diet it improved and kept on improving till it doesn't bother me at all now. This I can only describe as a miracle. After eight weeks, I went over to the maintenance diet but found I still wasn't happy with more fat so had a word with my doctor. He said: 'Don't worry about having more fat. You are obviously 100% better so stay with it and just increase bread, vegetables and fruit."

I am 70 this year and feel better now than for a few years past. I recommend the diet to everyone who's interested, but they have to buy their own book. I wouldn't part with mine for anything.

Everything you claimed for it has been *true* in my case and I can't thank you enough for it.

Wishing you every success in the future.'

## Indigestion

It was staggering to hear how many people had previously suffered from indigestion and heartburn, but who had found the symptoms disappear after following my diet. Here are just a small sample of the letters I received on this subject.

Elizabeth Hainworth wrote:

'Towards the end of last year I began to suffer from heartburn after every meal. The article about your diet appeared in the New Year, and I played around with it to start with, but after a binge on the cheese (my weakness) which brought on an attack of heartburn, I paid a visit to the doctor. He informed me I was overweight (1 st [6.4 kg]). Your diet was talked about and after that I stuck to it rigidly. Providing I watch the fat content on products the heartburn has virtually disappeared.'

Elizabeth lost 1 st 2 lbs (7.3 kg) in the following eight weeks.

Veronica Jarvis explained that she had been plagued with heartburn for the past two years, 'but not a sign of it these past eight weeks,' she said. And Carol Howes wrote on her questionnaire:

'I have dieted in the past, usually losing a pound or two (0.5 to 1 kg) then gaining three or four pounds (1 to 2 kg) and so my weight has steadily increased over the last eighteen years. I accepted the fact that I would just keep getting larger with age – albeit unhappily – and that, short of starvation, I would never be slim again.

My husband read of the Hip and Thigh Diet in the *Sunday Express* and said, "Here's a diet you can do." I was amazed, as this was the first time he'd openly admitted to me that he thought I was fat. "I couldn't do that," I said. "All that fruit would give me the runs!" However, I read it more closely and decided to give it a try. A previous diet with salads and fruit had upset my stomach so I was a little wary at first. One of my favourite fruits is an orange, but I just couldn't eat a whole one without trouble afterwards. This time I thought I'd give one a try and to my delight suffered no ill effects whatsoever and have eaten one a day ever since. The same goes for salads and other fruits – my stomach has never been so "settled".

The other wonderful effect is that I've had no inclination to eat sweets, cakes or chocolates and haven't binged for nearly three months. The past few weeks I've even bought chocolate and chocolate biscuits for the family and can sit and watch them being eaten without any desire for them myself – magic. I am so delighted with the smaller me, and have recommended the diet to family and friends – wishing I had shares in your publishers. Hubby seems quite chuffed too!

I intend to maintain this eating regime and stay slim.'

## Migraine

I can't begin to think how absolutely dreadful it must be to suffer from migraine. I grumble if I get a normal headache! I was aware of the benefits of the diet to migraine sufferers because Di Driver, one of my most successful followers of the diet in its original trial stage, was completely cured from this devastating condition after following the diet. I later learned of many more – both men and women. I was therefore not surprised when I began receiving more letters telling me of others' successes in this direction.

Mrs P. Crisp wrote:

'I have suffered cruelly from migraine since 1974 when my husband died, and I know chocolate, hard cheese, oranges and sometimes even wholemeal bread will bring on an attack, but since I went on your diet the attacks have virtually ceased. My dear mother suffered from this all her life but she adored fat on meat, bread, dripping and roast potatoes, and pre-war no one gave a thought to the idea that diet could help her. My doctor is delighted as it has meant far fewer tablets. This morning I had a try-on of summer skirts and slacks and my spirits have soared as my weight has gone down.'

Mrs Crisp, who is 5 ft 2 ins tall (1.57 m) and 70 years old, lost 16 lbs (7.3 kg) in ten weeks on the Hip and Thigh Diet and now weighs 9 st 8 lbs (61 kg).

Linda Goldsmith wrote:

'I am truly amazed by the results and it was so easy! Also my "sick" lethargic headaches seem to have disappeared almost completely. I can only put that down to not eating cream and rich food any more (very difficult as I am a hotelier by trade). I feel much better. My mother was so impressed at the way I look, she has also bought the book and started the diet.'

It's not surprising Linda's mother is impressed – Linda's vital statistics now read 33–26–36 (84–66–91 cm). She lost just 1 in (2.5 cm) from her bust, an amazing 4 ins (10 cm) from her waist and a total of 4 ins (10 cm) from her hips and widest part.

I believe the reason for the alleviation of migraine

symptoms is that only small amounts of dairy products are allowed in the diet. Also, of course, no chocolate is allowed and this is recognized as a 'baddie' for migraine sufferers.

## Pre-menstrual tension

Pre-menstrual tension (PMT) is frequently discussed in the media as it affects so very many women. I have absolutely no idea why my diet should help this condition, but I received several letters in which slimmers explained how their general health and well-being had improved significantly. The first hint was when I received the following letter from Barbara Jones:

'I have now been following your diet for three weeks and so far have lost 13 lbs (5.9 kg) in weight. I have followed many diets over the last ten years. Never have I lost so much so easily and quickly – I normally lose 1–1½ lbs (approx. 0.5 kg) per week. I have found the diet easy to follow and have never felt hungry. I have also been doing the exercises in your book, working out 2–3 times per week and playing squash. I have made some minor adjustments to the recipes shown, as I do not eat very much meat – only white turkey/chicken breast about twice a week. However, I find I can make very tasty meals with chick peas, kidney beans, etc.

As I have kept accurate measurements since Day 1, I should like to take part in your survey and complete the questionnaire.

I would also add that I feel very well following this diet and, as an added bonus, have not suffered from PMT this month, as I normally do.'

I sent Barbara a questionnaire which she returned after following the diet for eight weeks. By then she had lost 24 lbs (10.9 kg) and had reduced her inches magnificently: 3 ins (7.5 cm) off bust and waist, 4 ins (10 cm) from hips and widest part, and 2½ ins (6 cm) from each thigh. She added that her PMT symptoms had disappeared, 'and I feel great' she wrote.

Mrs Aileen Charley lost 18 lbs in eight weeks and ½ in from her bust, 2½ ins (6 cm) from her waist, 2 ins (5 cm) from her hips, 3 ins (7.5 cm) from her widest part, and an inch (2.5 cm) from each of her already-slim thighs (now 20 ins) [51 cm]. Aileen wrote:

> 'Since starting this diet I have noticed a great improvement during the week before my periods. My breasts are no longer sore and tender and instead of putting 5–6 lbs (approx 2.5 kg) on during that week I remain the same weight. The spots that used to appear on my face and neck during that week have also gone. I am still breast-feeding my four-year-old daughter so I'm afraid I drink more than ½ pint (250 ml) of semi-skimmed milk a day, but the pounds and inches are still coming off. It's lovely not to be "fat and forty" any more and it's even better being lighter than my 14-year-old son who is 6 ins taller than me.'

Pauline Perry wrote telling me that before her

monthly period she is usually bad tempered, 'but I feel less ratty than usual'. Pauline lost 19 lbs (8.6 kg) in eight weeks and lost a staggering 8 ins (20 cm) from her widest part.

Mrs B. S. wrote: 'As I mentioned in my letter dated 9th June your diet has helped me with a very painful problem, that of swollen breasts (as part of PMT). I have since been informed by my mother-in-law who is a GP, that this is one of the few symptoms of PMT that is untreatable, consequently I hope that many other women that suffer in this way, can find relief by cutting out fat from their diet.'

Mrs Jill Davies wrote: 'I have enjoyed this diet and the results are fantastic. Also I used to suffer from PMT. This has stopped. I liked this diet because the inches went from where I wanted them to go from.'

Jill lost nothing from her 34-in (86 cm) bust, 2½ ins (6 cm) from her waist, 6 ins (15 cm) from her hips, 5 ins (12.7 cm) from her widest part, 4½ ins (11 cm) from each thigh and 3 ins (8 cm) from just above each knee. Her vital statistics are now 34–25½–33 (86–65–84 cm).

## Pregnancy

Ava Richardson telephoned me shortly after my book was published. She was 26 weeks into her pregnancy and wanted to know if she could follow the diet. I recommended that she increase the allowance of milk and protein foods and should show her doctor the diet before commencing. Ava kept me up to date with her progress and condition throughout the remaining weeks. Despite the fact that she suffered from a back problem and had to rest for most of the time, she still managed to lose ¾ in (2 cm) from her hips and widest part, and over 1 in (2.5 cm) from each of her thighs. She told me that despite the fact that she stopped dieting some weeks before the baby was born, her inch losses were maintained despite the gain in her weight. When I spoke to Ava after Gregory Peter had been born (8 lbs 6 ozs) [3.8 kg] she said she felt wonderful and was now back on the diet to reduce her weight still further.

N.B. *Always* check with your doctor first before embarking on any diet during pregnancy.

## Underactive thyroid

A State Registered Nurse wrote to me explaining that she suffered from an underactive thyroid 'so everything was against me'. She continued:

'I would like to thank you for the diet which I am following with no trouble and seeing results already. It is marvellous.'

So if you are a sufferer, it is well worth a try. But do check with your doctor first.

# 6
# 'This diet changed my life!'

We all know that anyone who has to watch their weight feels much more confident when slim. Our outlook and attitude to life is totally different from how we feel when we are overweight. I would suggest that our mental attitude can change so dramatically for the better, that we are able actually to *achieve* more than we ever thought possible. Someone who is overweight often feels 'ugly' and subconsciously doesn't *want* to succeed, preferring to disappear into oblivion, hoping that the world will not notice them. But that same person, having successfully lost all their excess weight, becomes a completely different sort of person – creative, confident, positive. Now that person's *ability* won't have changed, but their *desire* to live life to the full will be dramatically increased.

Among the many letters I received this new mental attitude became very obvious. Catherine Ann Pike wrote:

'I would just like to take this opportunity to say thank you for writing a marvellous book and losing 3 st (19.1 kg) has certainly changed my life, making me more confident and very happy.'

Avril Daley wrote this on her questionnaire:

'My husband has also been on your diet and has lost 10 lbs. He feels so much better and has a lot more energy. So, I would like to thank you for introducing me to your diet; it has made such a difference to me. I have now started an Office Training Course for the unemployed and am learning to type and use a word processor. It has given me confidence to go back out to work and take a pride in myself once again, instead of sitting at home eating.'

Margaret Venables wrote to me and mentioned that she worked in a voluntary capacity with an international children's organization, meeting a lot of people at all levels. 'Never again will I feel like a stranded whale,' she said – which is exactly how so many overweight people feel when they are in public.

It doesn't help, of course, to have tried to slim for years and to have continually failed. Margaret explained her history of struggling:

'Previously I had been to Weight Watchers – good – expensive – and I soon put back the weight. The specialist sent me to the dietician at our Royal Infirmary and, despite being careful with what I ate, there was no obvious weight loss. My doctor said, "Stop eating", and he gave me tablets to help – again little weight loss and I began to feel at odds with myself.'

Margaret began the Hip and Thigh Diet at the end of January. Her letter continued:

'Yesterday was my third Sunday and I feel great – weight loss so far 5 lbs (2.3 kg). We had our daughter's twenty-first birthday party on Saturday and I still lost weight – 1½ ins (4 cm) from my bust, 1 in (2.5 cm) from my waist – but most important I feel great and your diet has given me back my interest in myself and that is amazing.

No doubt you receive many, many letters – but I just had to write and tell you how I felt.'

I replied to Margaret's letter and asked her to tell me about her progress. In April, Margaret wrote again and this is what she said:

'I am sending you my "loss" chart for the first eight weeks of my new eating habit.

I find it incredible that I have lost inches even though these eight weeks have included our daughter's twenty-first birthday celebrations, several trips to London for meetings, my own birthday and a parish lunch.

In the past, my efforts to diet have certainly resulted in the loss of a few pounds and I have watched the scales carefully – but the weight has rapidly returned and I have been back to square one. This new eating habit is so simple – once your palate has adjusted to the new tastes it ceases to be a diet, and I have never felt better.

You mentioned in your letter that you would like to quote me in your next book. If I can help anyone to improve their health, then please feel free to use my comments.'

Margaret's inch losses were totally satisfactory. Her

bust had reduced from 38 to 36 ins (96.5 to 91.5 cm), her waist had slimmed by 3½ ins (9 cm), hips by 1½ ins (4 cm) and each thigh had trimmed off 2 ins (5 cm). You can imagine how much more confident Margaret must have felt at the various functions she had attended – particularly her daughter's twenty-first birthday when any mother is conscious of her advancing years.

Another lady who asked to remain anonymous wrote:

'While I was following your diet, and ever since, I have felt so much healthier and, with the renewed confidence in my slimmer self, I feel great! Forgive me for mentioning this but the man in my life has commented on the change in me. He thinks it's his birthday whenever we get together!'

Yes, losing weight and feeling happier about your body certainly does make you feel a lot more contented about yourself when in a close relationship – whether you are simply dancing and not having to worry about your partner feeling folds of fat under your bra as he places his hands on your back, or whether you're making love.

Lorna Cowley, whose comments were reproduced in the first sentence of this book, wrote that losing weight and finding her confidence had completely revolutionized her life! Lorna's husband was unwell and unable to drive the family car. She had not driven for fifteen years but one day, quite amazingly, she decided to have a go. Living in the country and having a 'family' of animals to feed she discovered she had run low in pet foodstuffs. She took her courage in her hands and managed to drive to the local pet shop. 'I was really nervous,' she said. 'I didn't know where the indicators were and I simply forgot about the seat belt. When I got to the shop I had to ask a farmer to turn the car round for me so that I could drive home!'

Since then she has increased in confidence, drives regularly, even through large towns, and knows how to check the oil, battery, tyres and water. What an achievement!

Lorna wrote so enthusiastically about the positive changes in her life that she is a totally different sort of person – one she actually feels happy with.

'I am so *very* grateful for your fantastic diet, and really proud of my new trim figure for my age. I have found a super stylist for my hair. When I collected my very expensive new classic suit last week, I was told that if I slimmed down any more – it wouldn't fit me! I felt quite like a model in it!'

What a delightful transformation in attitude. Wonderful!

Perhaps the most dramatic transformation was experienced by Helen, who wrote to me on 20 March. This is what she said:

'THANK YOU!!!

*January 9* – went to sales, squeezing into size 16.
*January 10* – your diet was in *Sunday Express*. Started immediately.

Up to this date, no social life, very conscious of overweight. I'm 5 ft 6 ins (1.68 m) but felt so *fat*. Also, for long-engrained reasons, terrified of being hungry.
*March 19* – into size 12s. Confident enough to join Computer Dating Agency last week, all wanting to see me again.
*March 24* – Annual General Meeting at work. Surrounded by compliments. New hairstyle, make-up and glamorous specs.

I'm 49 this Thursday. The girls (average age 23) have grabbed your book and it sits in the office. If this sounds like an advert, too bad. I'm happy and without being hungry!'

In my reply, I requested permission to reproduce Helen's letter – and also asked her if she would like to complete a questionnaire. She wrote back:

'Thank you for your kind letter. I have filled in the questionnaire in a way you might not find typical. When you read my replies you will see why.

You have full permission to publish my initial letter and perhaps the other history. Nobody is unique and it could be worth a chapter – even some dieticians/shrinks might be interested. Anonymity isn't important.

Last night, a nice man (younger than me!) expressed beautiful remarks about me physically and proposed. I may not accept, but this is down to your basic sense in making it possible.

Seems as though life may begin at 49!

After a lifetime of eating disorders and totally abnormal attitudes to food, you have set me straight in two months. Mother would have apoplexy if she saw me now!'

When I read this letter, I could sense that Helen had gone through some very difficult times in her life. I could see how successful she had been in following the diet. At 5 ft 6 ins (1.68 m) tall and wearing size 8 shoes it was clear that Helen was large boned. In eleven weeks she had reduced her weight from 12 st 3 lbs to 9 st 6 lbs (77.7 to 60 kg). She had followed the diet extremely strictly, cutting out the bread and potatoes. This had not affected her health in any way and, she said, 'I feel wonderful and confident – run up stairs like a ten-year-old.'

Helen wanted to lose the heavy look on her face and she described the result: 'New face meant lovely new hairstyle – super make-up and new specs.'

She found the quick results and the encouragement she received from her work colleagues enabled her to enjoy following the diet. She hardly ever felt hungry and 'above all I can live sensibly with meals out as wanted'. She often used to binge, but never did whilst following the Hip and Thigh Diet.

In answer to the question: 'Were you more successful on this diet than with previous diets?' Helen ticked YES, with six ticks! 'I didn't feel hungry, of which I have a horror – see below,' she wrote. Then she told me about her tragic earlier life.

'*Age 10–16* – Mother starved me. She hated father, said he was all she could get because she was fat when young. At 10, I was attacked for "stealing" slice of bread. Public weighings at Boots with hysterical outbursts if up 4 ozs (100 g). Friends at school pitied me.

*Age 16–31* – Kept severely 'controlled'. Her sadism was matched by ignorance. Simultaneously 'protected' from young men, my being saved for her old age. Food was heaven when I got it.

*Age 31* – Left home, orgy of eating.

*Age 40* – Still all potential husbands manipulated off. Career brilliant. 15 st (95.4 kg), crash dieted on diet of Coke/black coffee.

*Age 40 + 8 months* – 8½ st (54 kg).

*Age 40–48* – Alternated anorexia and bulimia – down to under 7 st (44.5 kg). (By now unable to sustain hunger.) In and out of hospital. Career in limbo as tied to mother.

*Age 48* – Broke from mother. Bingeing, new happy job, content, undisciplined about eating – cheese, butter, etc. Feeling unattractive. Size 16+.

*Age 48+* – January 10 Sales, size 16+.
January 11 Started diet.
(Eating now a nice normal feature, not a career!)
March 9   Shopped, size 12. Enrolled in marriage bureau.
March 24  49th birthday.
March 26  First proposal – and now found sexually desirable.

I am happy. Flat being renovated like me! *Life is great!*'

# 7
# Thighs of Relief – Hip, Hip, Hooray!

*What the questionnaires told me*

I can remember the sheer joy I felt when, after the first trial of the diet, the completed questionnaires began dropping through my letter box. The air of enthusiasm and excitement from the trial team spurred me on tremendously as I wrote my first Hip and Thigh Diet book.

You can imagine my delight when again, after the book was published, people started writing to tell me how successful they had found the diet. I had never considered writing a follow-up Hip and Thigh Diet book, but as time went by and more ideas for meals were requested it became clear that a follow-up was inevitable, plus a cookery book, exercise cassette and video!

Another questionnaire needed to be issued to anyone who would be kind enough to complete one. Very conveniently we have a computer company located next door to us and they prepared a document which drew out comprehensive statistical information in a very readable and understandable format.

This chapter details the results of these completed questionnaires which were offered to everyone who wrote – for whatever reason – in fact, to anyone who had followed the diet seriously for at least eight weeks. 350 questionnaires were issued and almost 200 were returned completed.

The initial analysis from which I commenced writing this second book was based on the results of 129 completed questionnaires. As my book approached completion I updated the statistics with the results from another 60 questionnaires which I had received in the meantime. It was fascinating to realize that the attitudes, opinions and results were virtually unchanged, though the number of responses had increased. This was excellent news, because it indicated that despite the number of volunteers who had kindly completed questionnaires being really quite small, the results were consistent and they were very interesting indeed.

The majority were completed by women in the middle age range, 35–64, falling in almost equal quantities into the 35–44, 45–54 and 55–64 age ranges. 15.8% described themselves as 'very overweight', 45.6% said they were 'quite overweight', 33.9% described themselves as 'slightly overweight' and 4.7% were 'not overweight' but wished to reduce inches.

The average time of following the diet was eight weeks and the average weight loss was 1 st (14 lbs [6.4 kg]). 49.7% said they followed the diet 'very strictly', 48.5% said 'moderately strictly', and 1.8% said 'not very strictly'.

I asked the computer to segregate the 'strict' slimmers and to calculate their average weight loss. Not surprisingly it was proved that those who followed the diet 'very strictly' lost an average of

16 lbs (7.3 kg) over the average eight-week period, with those who followed it 'moderately strictly' losing 12 lbs (5.4 kg). Those who were following the diet 'not very strictly' still managed to lose 7 lbs (3.2 kg) over the average eight-week period.

Another aspect in which I was very interested was related to the fact that I had allowed a couple of alcoholic drinks per day to be consumed within the diet. We extracted from the computer those who said they had consumed their alcohol allowance *and* had followed the diet 'very strictly' and their average weight loss over eight weeks was *greater* at 17 lbs (7.7 kg). Well, would you believe it? They had lost 1 lb (0.454 kg) *more* than the average. We further investigated this question and discovered that the 'very strict' dieters who drank only occasionally lost an average of 16 lbs (7.3 kg) and those who were non-drinkers but stuck 'strictly' to the diet actually lost less, losing an average of 15 lbs (6.8 kg). Now I am not suggesting in any way that consuming alcohol will help you lose weight, but what I *do* think is that having a drink in the evening *can* have the effect of relaxing us, so we do not indulge in so much nervous nibbling. Watch out, though, that you don't get *so* relaxed that you abandon the diet altogether.

I have already, in chapter 3, detailed the inch loss statistics, and from which areas of the body dieters succeeded in slimming, so I will not repeat them, wonderful though the results were! Here are the answers to the other questions not mentioned elsewhere.

*Do you think your cellulite has reduced?* I asked.

A few didn't answer the question, but of the remainder, 55.5% said a definite 'Yes', 10.2% said 'No' and the remaining 34.3% said they didn't know.

Cellulite is the ghastly dimpled flesh only found on women (and not necessarily overweight women) around thighs, hips and upper arms. It is ugly because it gives an uneven appearance to the skin, creating actual cavities in the flesh if pinched; an 'orange-peel' effect is another term used to describe it. I had experienced a dramatic improvement on my own legs when I first embarked on my diet for health reasons. I used to call myself 'Miss Cellulite 198 . . .' according to the year! It was a constant source of real embarrassment. When I followed my very low fat diet, I didn't eliminate the presence of cellulite, but it was significantly improved. I was glad to see that so many Hip and Thigh Dieters had experienced similar results. Jo Hodgart, for example, wrote: 'I had *terrible* "orange-peel" thighs, but they are almost normal now.'

*Did you feel healthier as a result of following this diet?*

I was interested to know how people had felt since following my diet. A resounding 89% stated they felt healthier, with only 2% saying they didn't feel better, 9% said there was 'no change' in the way they felt.

In answer to the question *What was the effect of the diet on hair, nails and skin?* these were the results:

|       | *Improved* | *Deteriorated* | *Same* |
|-------|------------|----------------|--------|
| Hair  | 32.9%      | 1.6%           | 65.5%  |
| Nails | 26.9%      | 10.5%          | 62.6%  |
| Skin  | 33.9%      | 2.9%           | 63.2%  |

I think if you had asked anyone before embarking on the diet what the effects *might* have been, the answers would almost certainly have been 'deterioration' on all counts because we were changing our eating habits so dramatically. I was delighted with such a positive result: a far greater degree of *improvement*, compared with very little deterioration. This would seem to further confirm that the Hip and Thigh Diet really is a healthy one. Often we can experience a deterioration in the condition of our hair and skin within *days* if we are unwell. So to see such a degree of improvement in such a short period of time must be encouraging and comforting to anyone who has doubts. Helena Livingstone wrote:

'One thing I must thank you for is the massive improvement in my skin. It always used to be very dingy and blotchy but now it glows! So much so that people have actually commented upon it!'

I asked my slimmers if they enjoyed following this diet. Everyone, except one gentleman, answered YES. (I rather think he had been forced on to it by his wife. Oh dear!)

In answer to the question about alcohol consumption, 30.6% said they did drink their alcohol allowance of two drinks a day; 44.8% said they did 'occasionally', whilst 24.6% did not.

I asked if my volunteers had been following a diet before embarking on the Hip and Thigh Diet. 16.9% had been dieting recently but the remainder had not. 12.9% said it was their first attempt at dieting, 50.3% said they had dieted very occasionally in the past and 36.3% admitted trying more diets than they cared to remember! *An amazing 98.2% said they were more successful on this diet*; 1.8% said they were not more successful. Some, of course, abstained from answering the question because they had never dieted before.

So why was the Hip and Thigh Diet more successful? As we discussed in an earlier chapter, dieters said it was mainly because it was easy to follow; they could eat so much more than on most diets; because it didn't involve any calorie counting; and because they could *see* the results so quickly. A great number of the questionnaires I received included the spontaneous comment from slimmers that 'this didn't seem like a diet; it is more a way of eating'. I think that really sums up why it is so incredibly successful – diets fail because the slimmer feels over-disciplined, deprived and hungry. With the Hip and Thigh Diet you don't experience any of these feelings.

This was further proved by a separate trial which was organized by *The Journal* newspaper in Newcastle-Upon-Tyne. During my book promotional tour I had a very enjoyable interview with a charming lady called Avril Deane who is the Women's Page Editor. When she suggested her own trial, run through the newspaper, I couldn't help feeling that Avril was waiting for me to hesitate and question whether this was a good idea. Naturally, knowing how effective the diet was, I was all for putting it to the test yet again. *Journal* readers were asked to write in and twelve were selected to follow the diet, for eight weeks. I had no contact with them whatsoever.

In early June the following piece appeared in *The Journal*.

### *THIGHS OF RELIEF AND HIP HIP HOORAY!*

Words of praise from readers for writer Rosemary Conley and her Hip and Thigh Diet which we featured in February. . . .

The no-fat diet, specially for pear-shaped people, has helped them shed stones (many kilos) of unwanted weight and now they are persuading their friends to give it a go.

'I've lost a stone (6.4 kg) in eight weeks and I'm really pleased,' says Mrs Maureen Rumfitt, who was one of our dozen volunteers who agreed to try out the diet.

'I'm going on holiday soon and I'm keeping on with it until I reach the right weight. I've tried other diets and usually the weight has come straight off my bust.

Maureen, 42, and a mother of four grown up children, had despaired of losing weight on her thighs and hips.

For Mrs Sandra Kitching, 26, with a year-old daughter, the diet has helped her get down to her ideal size by getting rid of a surplus stone (6.4 kg).

'I lost the weight in six weeks and most of the time it was quite easy to stick to the diet.

Occasionally I fancied a bit of chocolate but there was plenty to eat and I certainly wasn't starving,' says Sandra who lives in Jarrow.

Capheaton postmistress Mrs Sheila Davidson managed to lose one stone and six pounds (9.1 kg) during the first eight weeks and is persevering to lose another stone (6.4 kg) at least.

Her downfall was nibbling sweets while she was working in the post office and she was delighted with the way she lost her desire for margarine and butter and other fats.

But she confesses: 'Although I haven't had many sweets I still miss slices of cake at the weekends especially when the kids are eating them.'

Detailed questionnaires filled in by our readers who have been trying out the diet are being sent to Rosemary Conley who has promised she will try and include them in her next book. Many thanks to you all!

At the time of writing this book, I had actually received only two questionnaires (apparently the trial team had been interviewed on the telephone for the article). The two volunteers who did write to me in time to be included were Alison Hall and Linda Towns. Alison wrote:

'I measured myself prior to diet, and sent details to Avril Deane. I felt if I had to measure myself, that would put me off going any further. I tried on all the clothes that I haven't been able to wear for at least two years, and found *that* a better incentive to carry on. This diet means I can concentrate on living my life, without the worry of "what can I have and what I can't" to eat. I can thoroughly recommend this diet to anyone overweight. This diet has certainly taught me a healthy way to eat, without the need for pills, etc., in order to lose weight.

Thank you, Rosemary.'

Alison lost 11 lbs (5 kg). She lost 2 ins (5 cm) from her bust, 3½ ins (9 cm) from her waist, 3 ins (8 cm) from her hips, 3 ins (7.5 cm) from one thigh and 2 ins (5 cm) from the other.

Linda Towns reduced her weight from 10 st 5 lbs to 8 st 9 lbs (66 to 55 kg) and said:

'I haven't been this weight for at least thirteen years. I'm going on holiday soon and I hope I can be good. I shall return to the diet after my holiday knowing at last I've found a diet that really works with not *too* great an effort.

Thank you!'

Along with her 24 lbs (10.9 kg) weight loss, Linda lost 2 ins (5 cm) from her bust, 4 ins (10 cm) from her waist, 4 ins (10 cm) from her hips and almost 3 ins (8 cm) from each thigh, 2 ins (5 cm) from her knees and over 1 inch (2.5 cm) from each arm. No wonder she was pleased!

# 8
# The Diet – extended version

The diet described in the following pages is based on the original diet followed by my initial trial team, amended to cater for the discerning tastes of those who followed it, and now extended to incorporate all possible social demands whether they be on economic grounds or the practical need of taking a packed lunch to work. In this book I have also catered for vegetarians.

This diet includes many new menu suggestions, but for your convenience I have also repeated all the menu suggestions from the first Hip and Thigh Diet. The result is a vast variety of food to satisfy every possible taste, for those with a large appetite, those with a tiny one, those who like cooking and those who like to keep it simple. As you become more familiar with the fat content of foods by studying the very comprehensive fat tables in Chapter 13 you will soon be able to formulate your own diet menus. I have included a list of strictly forbidden foods within this chapter to enable you to make a definite resolution (*before* you commence the diet) to ban them. If you are going to cheat and sneak bars of chocolate or packets of salted peanuts into your cupboard to eat when nobody's looking, you might as well give this book to somebody else. It has been *proved* that this diet will help you achieve the kind of figure-shape you never dreamed possible, but there is only one person in the world who can actually make it work for you – and that's YOU.

Perhaps the best news for slimmers is that this diet gives you a greater volume of food than any other reducing diet, and gives you lots of freedom. You are allowed three meals a day and a couple of alcoholic drinks too into the bargain! You will be staggered how quickly you see results, both in weight and inch loss, and this will encourage you to continue. The additional energy and generally healthier feeling that was enjoyed by so many of those who wrote to me, or completed questionnaires, showed they had a real sense of happiness and contentment. It was wonderful for me to read about it and no doubt tremendous for those who experienced such success.

Just think – this is almost certainly going to be the last time you ever have to diet! Can you imagine how wonderful that will be? So go for it! You've got nothing to lose but those inches.

## Diet instructions

Eat three meals a day, selecting one meal from the Breakfast, Lunch and Dinner menus listed. The dinner menus offer three courses. These may be broken up to provide a snack for later in the day if necessary, but try if possible to stick to the three-meals-a-day routine.

## Daily allowance
10 fl oz (250 ml) [½ pint] skimmed low fat milk
or 8 oz (200 ml) semi-skimmed milk
2 alcoholic drinks (optional)

## Diet notes
'Unlimited vegetables' includes potatoes as well as all other vegetables providing they are cooked and served without fat. Pasta, providing it is egg free and fat free, may be substituted for potatoes, rice or similar carbohydrate food.

'One piece of fruit' means one average apple or one orange, etc., or approximately 4 oz (100g) in weight, e.g. a 4 oz (100 g) slice of pineapple.

*Red meat:* Don't forget to restrict red meat to just two helpings a week.

Thin gravy may be taken with dinner menus providing it is made with gravy powder, not granules. Do not add meat juices from the roasting tin since these contain fat.

All yogurts should be the low calorie, low fat, diet brands. Cottage cheese should be the low fat variety.

Jacket potatoes are stated without a weight restriction. Use your own discretion in order to satisfy your appetite (see my comments in Chapter 2).

## Between-meal snacks
Chopped cucumber, celery, carrots, tomatoes and peppers may be consumed between meals if necessary.

## The diet

**Part 1**    Breakfasts:    *Cereal breakfasts*
*Fruit breakfasts*
*Cooked and continental breakfasts*

**Part 2**    Lunches:    *Fruit lunches*
*Packed lunches*
*Cold lunches*
*Hot lunches*

**Part 3**    Dinners:    *Starters*
*Main courses: non-vegetarian*
*Main courses: vegetarian*
*Additional notes for vegetarians*
*Desserts*
*Drinks*
*Sauces and dressings*

**Part 4**    Daily nutritional requirements

**Part 5**    The forbidden list

**Part 6**    The binge corrector menu

# Part 1: Breakfasts

*Select any one*

## Cereal breakfasts

The following may be served with skimmed milk from allowance and 1 teaspoon brown sugar if desired.

1. 1 oz (25g) porridge oats, made with water, served with 2 teaspoons of honey, no sugar.
2. Home-made muesli (see Recipe 1, page 137).
3. 1 oz (25 g) bran flakes or bran flakes with sultanas.
4. 1 oz (25 g) cornflakes, puffed rice, sugar flakes or rye and raisin cereal.
5. 2 Weetabix.
6. 1 oz (25g) whole wheat cereal.

## Fruit breakfasts

N.B. 'Diet yogurt' means low fat, low calorie yogurt.

1. 1 banana plus 5 oz (150 g) diet yogurt – any flavour.
2. 4 oz (100 g) tinned peaches in natural juice plus 5 oz (150 g) diet yogurt – any flavour.
3. 5 prunes in natural juice plus 5 oz (150 g) natural diet yogurt.
4. 5 prunes in natural juice plus half a slice of toast plus 1 teaspoon marmalade.
5. 4 dried apricots, soaked, (see Recipe 2, page 137) plus 5 oz (150 g) diet yogurt – any flavour.
6. As much fresh fruit as you can eat at one sitting.
7. 5 oz (150 g) stewed fruit (cooked without sugar) plus diet yogurt – any flavour.
8. 6 oz (175 g) fruit compote (e.g. oranges, grapefruit, peaches, pineapple, pears – all in natural juice).
9. 8 oz (225 g) tinned grapefruit in natural juice.
10. 1 whole fresh grapefruit plus 5 oz (150 g) diet yogurt – any flavour.

## Cooked and continental breakfasts

1. 8 oz (225 g) baked beans served on 1 slice (1 oz) [25 g] toast.
2. 8 oz (225 g) tinned tomatoes served on 1 slice (1½ oz) [37 g] toast.
3. 2 oz (50 g) very lean bacon (all fat removed) served with unlimited tinned tomatoes.
4. Half a grapefruit, plus 1 slice (1½ oz) [37 g] toast with 2 teaspoons marmalade.
5. 8 oz (225 g) smoked haddock, steamed in skimmed milk.
6. 2 oz (50 g) lean ham, 2 tomatoes, plus 1 fresh wholemeal roll.
7. 2 oz (50 g) cured chicken or turkey breast, 2 tomatoes, plus 1 fresh wholemeal roll.
8. 2 oz (50 g) smoked turkey breast, plus 1 fresh wholemeal roll.
9. 1 oz (25 g) very lean bacon (all fat removed) served with 4 oz (100 g) mushrooms cooked in vegetable stock, 3 oz (75 g) baked beans, 8 oz (225 g) tinned tomatoes or 4 fresh tomatoes grilled.
10. 1 oz (25 g) very lean bacon (all fat removed), 4 oz (100 g) mushrooms cooked in stock, 8 oz (225 g) tinned tomatoes or 4 fresh tomatoes grilled, plus half a slice (¾ oz) [18 g] toast.

## Part 2: Lunches

*Select any one*

### Fruit lunches

1. Pineapple Boat (see Recipe 3, page 138).
2. Prawn and Grapefruit Cocktail (see Recipe 4, page 138).
3. 4–5 pieces any fruit (e.g. 1 orange, 1 apple, 1 pear, 4 oz [100 g] plums).
4. 8 oz (200 g) fresh fruit salad topped with 5 oz (150 g) low fat yogurt.
5. 2 pieces any fresh fruit plus 2 × 5 oz (2 × 150 g) diet yogurts.

## Packed lunches

1. 2 slices of bread, spread with reduced-oil salad dressing, piled with lettuce, salad and prawns.
2. Contents of small tin of baked beans, plus chopped salad of lettuce, tomatoes, onions, celery, cucumber.
3. 2 slices of bread with 1 oz (25 g) ham, 1 tomato and pickle.
4. 4 Ryvitas spread with 2 oz (50 g) pickle and 4 slices of turkey roll or chicken roll, or 3 oz (75 g) ordinary chicken or turkey breast plus 2 tomatoes. 1 piece of fruit.
5. Chicken leg (no skin), chopped salad (lettuce, tomatoes, onions, celery, cucumber), soy sauce or Worcestershire sauce plus natural yogurt.
6. 4 Ryvitas, low fat cottage cheese, topped with prawns.
7. 4 Ryvitas, spread thinly with Shape low fat soft cheese and topped with salad.
8. 4 oz (100 g) red kidney beans, 4 oz (100 g) sweetcorn, plus chopped cucumber, tomatoes, onions tossed in mint sauce and natural yogurt.
9. 4 × 5 oz (4 × 150 g) low fat, low calorie yogurts – any flavour.
10. Salad of lettuce, tomato, cucumber, onion, grated carrot, etc., plus prawns, shrimps, cockles, lobster or crab (6 oz [175 g] total seafood) and Seafood Dressing (see Recipe 5, page 139).

**cont.**

## Packed lunches cont.

11. 4 Ryvitas, spread with any flavour low fat cottage cheese, topped with tomatoes plus unlimited salad vegetables.
12. 1 slimmers' cup-a-soup. 2 Ryvitas with low fat cottage cheese or soft cheese topped with salad vegetables. 5 oz (150 g) diet yogurt.
13. 1 cup of slimmers' cup-a-soup. 2 pieces fresh fruit. 5 oz (150 g) diet yogurt.
14. 1 cup of slimmers' cup-a-soup. 1 thin slice of bread, spread with a teaspoon of reduced-oil salad dressing and topped with salad and ¼ oz (6 g) grated low fat cheddar, e.g. Shape or Tendale.
15. Triple decker sandwich – with 3 slices light bread (e.g. Nimble) filled with 1 oz (25 g) turkey or chicken breast roll, or 2 oz (50 g) cottage cheese, lettuce, tomatoes, cucumber, sliced Spanish onion. Spread bread with oil-free sweet pickle of your choice, e.g. Branston or similar, or mustard, ketchup or reduced oil salad dressing.
16. 3 Ryvitas spread with 2 oz (50 g) pilchards in tomato sauce, topped with sliced tomato.
17. 2 slices wholemeal bread, spread with Seafood Dressing (see Recipe 5, page 139) made into sandwiches with 2 oz (50 g) tinned salmon and cucumber.
18. 1 Pot Rice plus 5 oz (150 g) diet yogurt.

**Packed lunches cont.**

19. 4 slices wholemeal Nimble or similar light bread made into jumbo sandwiches. Spread bread with reduced-oil salad dressing and fill with lots of salad vegetables, e.g. lettuce, cucumber, onion, cress, tomatoes, beetroot, green and red peppers.
20. Rice salad: a bowl of chopped peppers, tomatoes, onion, peas, sweetcorn and cucumber mixed with cooked (boiled) brown rice and served with soy sauce.

## Cold lunches

1. Curried Chicken and Yogurt Salad (see Recipe 6, page 139).
2. Seafood Salad (see Recipe 7, page 139).
3. Cheese, Prawn and Asparagus Salad (see Recipe 8, page 140).
4. Chicken joint (with skin removed) or prawns, served with a chopped salad of lettuce, cucumber, radish, spring onions, peppers, tomatoes, with soy sauce or Yogurt Dressing (see Recipe 9, page 140).
5. Crab and asparagus open sandwiches: 2 slices wholemeal bread spread with Seafood Dressing (see Recipe 5, page 139). Spread fresh or tinned crab meat or seafood sticks on to the bread and decorate with asparagus spears.
6. Orange and Carrot Salad (see Recipe 10, page 141).
7. Red Kidney Bean Salad (see Recipe 11, page 141).
8. 4 oz (100 g) cottage cheese (any flavour) served with large assorted salad and Carrot Salad (see Recipe 12, page 142).
9. Large salad served with prawns, plus Carrot Salad (see Recipe 12, page 142) dressed with low fat natural yogurt.
10. 8 oz (225 g) carton low fat cottage cheese, with two tinned pear halves, chopped apple and celery, served on a bed of lettuce and garnished with tomato and cucumber.

## Cold lunches cont.

11. 3 oz (75 g) pilchards in tomato sauce, served with a large salad, and oil-free Orange and Lemon Vinaigrette dressing (see Recipe 13, page 142).
12. 3 oz (75 g) salmon served with a large salad and mint yogurt dressing.
13. Mixed salad served with 4 oz (100 g) diet coleslaw, e.g. Shape – any flavour, plus 4 oz (100 g) diet (Shape) potato salad, plus 2 oz (50 g) prawns or 2 oz (50 g) chicken.
14. 4 Ryvitas spread with low calorie coleslaw, any flavour, e.g. Shape, and topped with salad.

## Hot lunches

1. Pea and Ham Soup (see Recipe 14, page 142).
2. Jacket potato topped with 8 oz (225 g) can baked beans.
3. 2 slices wholemeal toast with 16 oz (450 g) tin baked beans.
4. Jacket potato served with low fat cottage cheese and salad (cottage cheese may be flavoured with chives, onion, pineapple, etc. but it must be 'low fat').
5. Baked stuffed apples (one or two) filled with 1 oz (25 g) dried fruit, a few breadcrumbs and sweetened with honey or artificial sweetener, served with plain low fat yogurt.
6. Clear or vegetable soup, served with one slice of toast followed by 2 pieces fresh fruit.
7. Jacket potato with 1 oz (25 g) roast beef, pork or ham (with all fat removed) or 2 oz (50 g) chicken (no skin), served with Branston pickle and salad.
8. 2 slices wholemeal toast with small tin baked beans and small tin tomatoes.
9. Jacket potato (see Recipe 79, page 188) served with sweetcorn and chopped salad.
10. Jacket potato served with grated carrot, chopped onion, tomatoes, sweetcorn and peppers, topped with natural yogurt.
11. Jacket potato filled with 4 oz (100 g) cottage cheese mixed with 4 teaspoons tomato purée and black pepper to taste.

**Hot lunches cont.**

12. Jacket potato with 4 oz (100 g) pot of Shape prawn coleslaw.
13. Jacket potato with 4 oz (100 g) Shape coleslaw.
14. Jacket potato with 4 oz (100 g) Shape 1000 Island coleslaw.
15. Jacket potato with 4 oz (100 g) Shape Garlic and Herb coleslaw.
16. Jacket Potato with Barbecue Sauce (see Recipe 15, page 143).
17. Jacket Potato with Chicken and Peppers (see Recipe 16, page 143).
18. Jacket Potato with Chopped Vegetables and yogurt dressing (see Recipe 17, page 144).
19. Jacket Potato with Prawns and Sweetcorn (see Recipe 18, page 144).
20. 2 oz (50 g) Diet Burger (vegetarian), served with large salad.

# Part 3: Dinners

*Select any one from each category:*
*Starters*
*Main courses*
*(vegetarian or non-vegetarian)*
*Desserts*

**Starters**

1. Crudités (see Recipe 19, page 145).
2. Chicken and Mushroom Soup (see Recipe 20, page 145).
3. Orange and Grapefruit Cocktail (see Recipe 21, page 146).
4. Melon and Prawn Salad (see Recipe 22, page 146).
5. Pair of Pears (see Recipe 23, page 147).
6. French Tomatoes (see Recipe 24, page 147).
7. Grapefruit segments in natural juice.
8. Melon balls in slimline ginger ale.
9. Clear soup.
10. Garlic Mushrooms (see Recipe 25, page 148).
11. Melon Salad (see Recipe 26, page 149).
12. Ratatouille (see Recipe 27, page 150).
13. Wedge of melon.
14. Half a grapefruit.
15. Grilled Grapefruit (see Recipe 28, page 150).

## Main courses: non-vegetarian

1. Stir-fried Chicken and Vegetables (see Recipe 29, page 151).
2. Haddock Florentine (see Recipe 30, page 151) with unlimited vegetables.
3. Chicken Veronique (see Recipe 31, page 152) with Lyonnaise Potatoes (see Recipe 32, page 154) and unlimited vegetables.
4. Tandoori Chicken (see Recipe 33, page 154).
5. Shepherds' Pie (see Recipe 34, page 155).
6. Fish Curry with rice (see Recipe 35, page 156).
7. Steak Surprise (see Recipe 36, page 157) plus jacket potato, boiled mushrooms, and unlimited vegetables.
8. 8 oz (225 g) steamed, grilled or microwaved white fish (cod, plaice, whiting, haddock, lemon sole, halibut) served with unlimited boiled vegetables.
9. 8 oz (225 g) chicken joint (weighed cooked including the bones), baked with skin removed, in Barbecue Sauce (see Recipe 37, page 157) and served with jacket potato or boiled brown rice and vegetables of your choice.
10. Scous (see Recipe 38, page 158).
11. Spaghetti Bolognese (see Recipe 39, page 159).
12. Barbecued Chicken or Turkey Kebabs (see Recipe 40, page 160) served with boiled brown rice.
13. 3 oz (75 g) roast leg of pork with all fat removed, served with apple sauce and unlimited vegetables.

**cont.**

## Main courses: non-vegetarian cont.

14. Steamed or grilled or microwaved trout, stuffed with prawns and served with a large salad or assorted vegetables.
15. 6 oz (175 g) calves' or lamb's liver, braised with onions, and served with unlimited vegetables.
16. 6 oz (175 g) turkey (no skin) served with cranberry sauce, dry roast potatoes, and unlimited vegetables.
17. 3 oz (75 g) roast lamb with all fat removed, served with Dry-roast Parsnips (see Recipe 82, page 190) and unlimited vegetables.
18. 6 oz (175 g) chicken (no skin) steamed, grilled, baked or microwaved, and served with unlimited vegetables.
19. Chicken or Prawn Chop Suey (see Recipe 41, page 161) served with boiled brown rice.
20. Chicken Curry (see Recipe 43, page 162) served with boiled brown rice.
21. 3 oz (75 g) grilled or baked gammon steak or gammon rashers, with all fat removed, served with pineapple and unlimited vegetables.
22. Fish Pie (see Recipe 44, page 163) served with unlimited vegetables.
23. 2 oz (50 g) bacon grilled, with all fat removed, served with grilled tomatoes, baked beans and jacket or boiled potatoes.
24. 4 oz (100 g) roast duck (all skin removed) served with unlimited vegetables.
25. Chinese Chicken (see Recipe 45, page 164).
26. Fish Risotto (see Recipe 46, page 165).

## Main courses: vegetarian

1. Stuffed Marrow (see Recipe 47, page 166) served with unlimited vegetables.
2. Vegetable Bake (see Recipe 48, page 166).
3. Vegetarian Shepherds' Pie (see Recipe 50, page 168) served with unlimited vegetables.
4. Vegetable Curry (see Recipe 51, page 169) served on a bed of boiled brown rice.
5. Vegetarian Chilli con Carne (see Recipe 52, page 169) served on a bed of boiled brown rice.
6. Vegetable Chilli (see Recipe 53, page 170) served on a bed of boiled brown rice.
7. Vegetarian Spaghetti Bolognese (see Recipe 54, page 171).
8. Mushroom Stroganoff (see Recipe 55, page 172) served with unlimited vegetables.
9. Bean Salad (see Recipe 56, page 172) served with cold boiled brown rice and soy sauce.
10. Hummus with Crudités (see Recipe 57, page 173).
11. Spiced Bean Casserole (see Recipe 58, page 174) served with unlimited vegetables.
12. Vegetable Kebabs (see Recipe 59, page 175) served on a bed of rice and sweetcorn.
13. Vegetable Casserole (see Recipe 60, page 176) served with boiled brown rice or Lyonnaise Potatoes (see Recipe 32, page 154).

**cont.**

## Main courses: vegetarian cont.

14. Three Bean Salad (see Recipe 61, page 177) served with salad and cold boiled brown rice.
15. Stuffed Peppers (see Recipe 62, page 177) served with salad.
16. Black Eye Bean Casserole (see Recipe 63, page 178).
17. Chick Pea and Fennel Casserole (see Recipe 64, page 179).
18. Vegetable Chop Suey (see Recipe 42, page 162) served with boiled brown rice.
19. Vegetarian Goulash (see Recipe 49, page 167).
20. Quarterpounder (100 g) Diet Burger, served with unlimited vegetables or large wholemeal bap.

## Additional notes for vegetarians

Vegetarians may include the following foods within menus designed by themselves or amended from the non-vegetarian dishes listed.

1 egg – 3 times a week.
1 oz (25 g) Shape Edam cheese on non-egg days. (ordinary Edam should not be used)
OR
1 oz (25 g) Shape Brie (ordinary Brie should not be used)

The following pulses may be eaten freely in your own recipes. Generally speaking, try not to exceed 6 oz (175 g) cooked weight per portion of pulses.

| | |
|---|---|
| Black eye beans | Haricot beans |
| Butter beans | Lentils |
| Chick peas | Mung beans |
| Continental lentils | Red kidney beans |
| Green split peas | Yellow split peas |

## Desserts

1. Meringue basket filled with raspberries and topped with raspberry yogurt.
2. Fruit Sundae (see Recipe 65, page 179).
3. Stuffed apple served with plain yogurt.
4. 4 oz (100 g) fresh fruit salad mixed with 4 oz (100 g) natural yogurt.
5. Stewed fruit (cooked without sugar) served with 3 oz (75 g) Low Fat Custard (see Recipe 66, page 180).
6. Apple and Blackcurrant Whip (see Recipe 67, page 180).
7. Pineapple and Orange Sorbet (see Recipe 68, page 181).
8. Raspberry Mousse (see Recipe 69, page 181).
9. Sliced banana topped with raspberry yogurt.
10. Fresh strawberries or raspberries served with diet yogurt.
11. Pears in Red Wine (see Recipe 70, page 182).
12. Pineapple in Kirsch (see Recipe 71, page 183).
13. Oranges in Cointreau (see Recipe 72, page 183).
14. Sliced banana topped with fresh raspberries or strawberries.
15. Fresh peaches sliced and served with fresh raspberries.
16. Two pieces of fruit of your choice.
17. Pineapple Boat (see Recipe 3, page 138).
18. Diet Rice Pudding (see Recipe 73, page 184).

## Desserts cont.

19. Fruit Sorbet (see Recipe 74, page 185).
20. Pears in Meringue (see Recipe 75, page 186).
21. 8 oz (225 g) fresh fruit salad.
22. Diet yogurt, including French style set yogurt.
23. Stewed rhubarb sweetened with artificial sweetener, served with rhubarb diet yogurt.
24. Low fat fromage frais – e.g. Shape – any flavour.

## Drinks

Tea and coffee may be drunk freely if drunk black, or may be drunk white so long as skimmed milk allowance is not exceeded. Use artificial sweetener whenever possible in place of sugar.

You may drink two alcoholic drinks per day. One drink means a single measure of spirit, a glass of wine, or small glass of sherry or half a pint (250 ml) of beer or lager. Slimline mixers should always be used and these and 'Diet' drinks may be drunk freely.

You may drink as much water as you like; sparkling mineral water tastes wonderful.

Grape, apple, unsweetened orange, grapefruit, pineapple and exotic fruit juices may be drunk in moderation.

See recipes for delicious low calorie drinks on pages 195–198.

## Sauces and dressings

Sauces made without fat, and with low fat skimmed milk from the daily allowance, may be eaten in moderation. Thin gravy made with gravy powder, but not granules, may also be served with main courses. Marmite or Bovril may be used freely to add flavour to cooking and on bread. For salads select any of the fat free dressings (see recipes) and occasionally you can have the seafood dressing which has the closest taste to salad dressing, according to the menu selected. Soy and Worcestershire sauce, lemon juice or vinegar may be eaten freely.

## Part 4: Daily nutritional requirements

In selecting your menus, each day try to incorporate the following minimum quantities:

6 oz (175 g) protein food (fish, poultry, meat, cottage cheese, baked beans).
12 oz (350 g) vegetables (including salad).
12 oz (350 g) fresh fruit.
6 oz (175 g) carbohydrate (bread, cereals, potatoes, rice, pasta).
5 oz (150 g) low fat yogurt.
10 fl oz (250 ml) skimmed low fat milk or 8 oz (200 ml) semi-skimmed milk.

I would also suggest that one multivitamin tablet be taken daily to make doubly sure that you are getting all the vitamins you need.

## Part 5: The forbidden list

These foods are strictly forbidden whilst following the diet. Some will be reintroduced for the maintenance programme.

Butter, margarine, Flora, Gold, Outline, or any similar products
Cream, soured cream, whole milk, Gold Top, Silver Top, etc.
Lard, oil (all kinds), dripping, suet, etc.
Milk puddings of any kind except Diet Rice Pudding (see Recipe 73, page 184)
Fried foods of any kind
Fat or skin from all meats, poultry, etc.

**cont.**

## The forbidden list cont.

All cheese except low fat cottage cheese unless otherwise stated in the diet menus
Egg yolk (the whites may be eaten freely)
Fatty fish including mackerel, kippers, roll mop herrings, eels, herrings, sardines, bloater, tuna, sprats, and whitebait
All nuts except chestnuts
Sunflower seeds
Goose
All fatty meats
Meat products, e.g. Scotch eggs, pork pie, faggots, black pudding, haggis, liver sausage, pâté
All types of sausages
All sauces containing cream or whole milk or eggs, e.g. salad dressing, mayonnaise, French dressing, parsley sauce, cheese sauce, Hollandaise sauce. (Waistline dressing may only be used as stated in the diet menus)
Cakes, sweet biscuits, pastries, sponge puddings, etc.
Chocolate, toffees, fudge, caramel, butterscotch
Savoury biscuits and crispbreads (except Ryvita)
Lemon curd
Marzipan
Cocoa and cocoa products, Horlicks
Crisps
Cream soups
Avocado pears
Yorkshire Pudding
Egg products, e.g., quiches, egg custard, pancakes etc.

# Part 6: The binge corrector menu

Inevitably there will be occasions when you are invited to eat food which is forbidden on this diet. It could be a restaurant dinner, a formal occasion such as a wedding, or just a plain, simple party where the buffet offers a high fat menu. Buffets are the worst – definitely. The slimmer finds it almost impossible to control him or herself once (s)he has 'just tried one of these – one won't do any harm'. Yes, it will happen and when you've done it you'll wish you hadn't and want to know what you can do to correct it.

The Binge Corrector Diet detailed below *is only to be used for one day maximum* to undo the harm you have done on such an occasion. If you use it too often you will completely ruin your metabolic rate and will find the proper diet less effective.

### Breakfast
Wedge of melon.

### Lunch
Slimmers cup-a-soup.
Diet yogurt.

### Dinner
Large salad of lettuce, cucumber, tomato, sliced mushrooms, sliced onion, grated carrot, cabbage.
4 oz (100 g) baked beans OR 2 oz (50 g) chicken breast or 3 oz (75 g) cottage cheese.
Soy sauce.

### Supper
6 oz (175 g) tomato juice.

### Drinks
4 oz (100 g) skimmed milk for tea and coffee.
Unlimited Diet coke, slimline drinks, etc.

# My favourite breakfasts

*Recipe No.    Brief Description or Recipe title*

# My favourite lunch menus

*Recipe No.     Brief Description or Recipe title*

# My favourite starter menus

*Recipe No.*      *Brief Description or Recipe title*

# My favourite dinners – main courses

*Recipe No.    Brief Description or Recipe title*

# My favourite desserts

*Recipe No.*     *Brief Description or Recipe title*

# 9
# Recipes

## Recipe 1
## Home-made Muesli

*(Serves 1)*

½ oz (12.5 g) oats
½ oz (12.5 g) sultanas or ½ banana
2 teaspoons bran
1 eating apple – grated or chopped
milk from allowance or mixed with 3 oz (75 g) natural yogurt

Mix all ingredients together and add honey to taste if required.

Alternatively, mix all ingredients (except banana) the night before and leave to soak in skimmed milk.

## Recipe 2
## Stewed Apricots or Prunes

Soak dried fruit overnight in hot black tea and artificial sweetener to taste. Add a pinch of cinnamon if you wish.

## Recipe 3
## Pineapple Boat

*(Serves 2)*

1 medium-sized fresh pineapple
8 oz (225 g) seasonal fruit of your choice
10 oz (275 g) diet yogurt – any flavour
cherry or strawberry to decorate

Divide the pineapple into two halves from top to bottom. Do not cut away the leaves – they add to the decorative look. Cut away flesh with a grapefruit knife and cut this flesh into cubes, removing hard core.

Prepare other fruit – wash and cut into bite-sized pieces and mix with pineapple. Pile into hollowed-out pineapple halves and dress with yogurt.

Serve chilled and decorate with either a cherry or strawberry.

## Recipe 4
## Prawn and Grapefruit Cocktail

*(Serves 2)*

1 fresh grapefruit
6 oz (175 g) peeled prawns
5 oz (150 g) diet grapefruit yogurt
(natural yogurt can be used if preferred)

Peel grapefruit, removing all pith. Separate into segments and place in a dish.

Sprinkle on the fresh prawns and dress with yogurt.

## Recipe 5
## Seafood Dressing

(*Serves 2*)

2 tablespoons tomato ketchup
1 tablespoon reduced oil salad dressing (e.g. Waistline, Heinz Weight Watchers)
squeeze of lemon juice

Mix all ingredients together and use as allowed.

## Recipe 6
## Curried Chicken and Yogurt Salad

(*Serves 1*)

2 oz (50 g) chicken breast, cut into cubes
5 oz (150 g) carton natural diet yogurt
1 teaspoon curry powder
unlimited green salad vegetables

Mix yogurt and curry powder together and stir in cubes of cooked chicken.
Serve on a bed of fresh green salad vegetables.

## Recipe 7
## Seafood Salad

4 seafood sticks, chopped
2 oz (50 g) prawns
2 oz (50 g) crab (optional)
shredded lettuce
tomato quarters
cucumber twists

2 lemon quarters
seafood dressing (see Recipe 5, page 139)

Mix seafood ingredients together and place on bed of shredded lettuce. Garnish with tomato quarters, cucumber twists and lemon quarters.

## Recipe 8
## Cheese, Prawn and Asparagus Salad

(*Serves 2*)

4 oz (100 g) carton cottage cheese
6 oz (175 g) peeled prawns
4 tablespoons chopped and diced cucumber
unlimited lettuce or watercress
8 oz (225 g) can asparagus tips
freshly ground black pepper

Mix the cottage cheese, prawns and cucumber together, seasoning to taste with the pepper.

Lay the mixture on a bed of shredded lettuce or watercress, and decorate with the asparagus tips.

## Recipe 9
## Yogurt Dressing

5 oz (150 g) natural yogurt
good squeeze lemon juice
salt
freshly ground black pepper

Mix all the ingredients together and serve as a dressing for salad.

## Recipe 10
## Orange and Carrot Salad

(*Serves 1*)

1 large orange
green salad vegetables (e.g. lettuce, cucumber, onion, cabbage, chicory, endives)
4 oz (100 g) low fat cottage cheese
4 oz (100 g) grated carrot

Remove peel and pith from orange and slice flesh into rounds. Arrange orange flesh on a bed of chopped green salad vegetables from the list above.

Place the cottage cheese in the centre, piling grated carrot on top. Dress with Oil-free Orange and Lemon Vinaigrette (see Recipe 13).

## Recipe 11
## Red Kidney Bean Salad

(*Serves 1*)

8 oz (225 g) red kidney beans, cooked
4 oz (100 g) potato, cooked and chopped
3 oz (75 g) peas, cooked
onion rings, fresh
5 oz (150 g) natural yogurt
green salad vegetables
chopped mint, if available

Mix the beans, peas, potato and mint with the yogurt and serve on a bed of salad vegetables. Decorate with onion rings.

## Recipe 12
### Carrot Salad

(*Serves 1*)

2 large fresh carrots, peeled
1 oz (25 g) sultanas

Grate carrots and mix with the sultanas. Serve with a salad or on a jacket potato.

## Recipe 13
### Oil-free Orange and Lemon Vinaigrette

4 oz (100 g) wine vinegar
4 tablespoons lemon juice
4 tablespoons orange juice
grated rind of one lemon
½ teaspoon French mustard
pinch garlic salt
freshly ground black pepper

Place all the ingredients in a bowl and mix thoroughly. Keep in a refrigerator and use within two days.

## Recipe 14
### Pea and Ham Soup

(*Serves 4*)

1 onion, peeled and sliced
1 lb (450 g) gammon pieces (weighed after fat cut off)
1 lb (450 g) potatoes, peeled and quartered
4 oz (100 g) dried peas (soaked overnight)

2–3 pints (1 to 1.7 litres) water
mixed herbs

Bring gammon and onion to boil, and simmer for one hour. Cool and skim. Bring to the boil again; add potatoes and peas, and simmer gently for 1–2 hours. A tiny pinch of mixed herbs adds flavour.

The longer this is cooked, the thicker it becomes.

## Recipe 15
## Jacket Potato with Barbecue Sauce

(*Serves 1*)

1 teaspoon Worcestershire sauce
1 tablespoon brown sauce
1 tablespoon tomato ketchup
1 tablespoon mushroom sauce
Prawns or cooked chicken (3 oz) [75 g] if desired
1 cooked jacket potato

Heat the sauces in a small non-stick saucepan. Add prawns or chicken if desired and heat thoroughly.

Serve on the jacket potato.

## Recipe 16
## Jacket Potato with Chicken and Peppers

(*Serves 1*)

2 oz (50 g) cooked chicken flesh
¼ red and green peppers (raw), deseeded and chopped
1 tablespoon natural yogurt
1 tablespoon reduced-oil salad dressing
salt and freshly ground black pepper
1 cooked jacket potato

Mix the first five ingredients together and add the contents of the jacket potato.

Pile back into the 'jacket' and reheat in the oven for 5 minutes.

## Recipe 17
## Jacket Potato with Chopped Vegetables

(*Serves 1*)

½ green and red pepper (raw)
1 oz (25 g) sweetcorn
½ chopped onion (raw)
2 mushrooms (raw), chopped
1 oz (25 g) chopped cucumber
2 tablespoons natural yogurt
salt and freshly ground black pepper
1 cooked jacket potato, halved and opened

Mix the first seven ingredients together and pile on to the two halves of the jacket potato. Serve immediately.

## Recipe 18
## Jacket Potato with Prawns and Sweetcorn

(*Serves 1*)

2 oz (50 g) prawns
2 oz (50 g) sweetcorn
1 tablespoon reduced-oil salad dressing
1 tablespoon tomato ketchup
salt and freshly ground black pepper to taste
1 cooked jacket potato, halved and opened

Mix the first five ingredients together and pile on

to the two halves of the jacket potato. Serve immediately.

## Recipe 19
## Crudités

Sticks and sprigs of raw cucumber, carrots, celery, green and red peppers and cauliflower, served with Garlic or Mint Yogurt Dip (see Recipe 77, page 188).

## Recipe 20
## Chicken and Mushroom Soup

*(Serves 4)*

bones of one chicken
2 pints (1 litre) vegetable stock (water from cooking vegetables)
1 chicken stock cube
1 onion, sliced
1 carrot, sliced
1 teaspoon mixed herbs
sprinkling of garlic salt if desired
black pepper to taste
1 bay leaf
6 peppercorns
4 oz (100 g) mushrooms, washed and sliced

Place all ingredients except mushrooms in a large saucepan and cover. Bring to the boil and simmer for approximately 2–3 hours. Taste. If too weak, boil a little faster and remove the saucepan lid until liquid has reduced and it tastes appetizing. Strain away bones and vegetables.

Replace soup in saucepan, add sliced mushrooms, cover and cook for 10 minutes.

Serve piping hot.

## Recipe 21
## Orange and Grapefruit Cocktail

(*Serves 2*)

1 large orange
1 grapefruit

Remove all peel and pith from both fruits. Work the segments from core with a sharp knife and arrange in two dishes. Squeeze as much juice as possible on to the fruit from the peel and core.

Serve chilled.

## Recipe 22
## Melon and Prawn Salad

(*Serves 2*)

1 melon
4 oz (100 g) prawns

Halve the melon and remove seeds. Scoop out flesh of melon with a ball-scoop. Mix the melon balls carefully with the shelled prawns, and replace in empty melon shells. Serve chilled.

## Recipe 23
## Pair of Pears

(*Serves 1*)

1 ripe pear
4 oz (100 g) low fat cottage cheese
lemon juice
shredded lettuce

Peel, halve lengthways, and core a ripe pear, and paint with lemon juice to prevent discoloration. Fill cavities with low fat cottage cheese and serve on a bed of shredded lettuce.

## Recipe 24
## French Tomatoes

French tomatoes are so called because in the traditional recipe Gervais Cream Cheese is used in place of the low fat cottage cheese.

8 tomatoes
salt and pepper
6 oz (175 g) low fat cottage cheese
small bunch of fresh chives, chopped spring onion tops or parsley
watercress to garnish
oil-free vinaigrette dressing (see Recipe 88, page 193)

Scald and skin the tomatoes by placing them in a bowl, pouring boiling water over them, counting to fifteen before pouring off the hot water and replacing it with cold. The skin then comes off easily.

Cut a slice from the non-stalk end of each tomato and reserve slices. Hold tomato in the palm of your hand and remove seeds with the handle of a teaspoon, then remove the core with the bowl of the spoon. Drain the hollowed out tomato and season lightly inside each one with salt.

Soften cheese with a fork and when soft add finely chopped chives, parsley or spring onion tops and season well. Fill the tomatoes with the cheese mixture, using a small teaspoon, until the mixture is above the rim of the tomato. Replace their top slices on the slant and arrange them in a serving dish.

Make dressing (see Recipe 88, page 193) and spoon over the tomatoes, saving some to add just before serving. Chill tomatoes for up to 2 hours. Before serving, garnish with watercress and sprinkle remaining chives and dressing over tomatoes.

## Recipe 25
## Garlic Mushrooms

(*Serves 4*)

1 lb (450 g) button mushrooms
½ pint (250 ml) chicken stock
3 cloves fresh garlic
salt and pepper

Wash mushrooms and drain. Heat chicken stock with peeled and finely shredded garlic cloves. Boil for 5 minutes on gentle heat then add mushrooms and simmer in a covered saucepan for a further 7 minutes.

Serve in soup dishes and eat with a spoon.

## Recipe 26
## Melon Salad

*(Serves 4)*

1 honeydew melon
1 lb (450 g) tomatoes
1 large cucumber
salt
1 tablespoon parsley
1 heaped teaspoon mint and chives (chopped)
oil-free vinaigrette dressing (see Recipe 88, page 193)

Cut the melon in half, remove the seeds and scoop out the flesh; a curved grapefruit knife is useful for this, if you have one. Cut the flesh into cubes.

Skin and quarter the tomatoes, squeeze out the seeds and remove the core; cut quarters again if the tomatoes are large.

Peel the cucumber, cut into small cubes about the same size as the melon cubes. Sprinkle with salt, cover with a plate and stand for 30 minutes. Drain away any liquid and rinse cubes in cold water.

Mix the fruit and vegetables together in a deep bowl. Pour over the dressing; cover and chill for 2–3 hours. Just before serving, mix in the herbs.

As the salad makes a lot of juice it should be eaten with a spoon. A Hot Herb Loaf (Recipe 90, page 193) goes well with melon salad.

## Recipe 27
### Ratatouille

*(Serves 2)*

½ lb (225 g) courgettes
2 aubergines
1 large green pepper
2 small onions (finely sliced into rings)
15 oz (425 g) tin of tomatoes
2 cloves garlic (chopped) – optional
2 bay leaves
freshly ground black pepper
salt

Slice the courgettes and aubergines. Halve the pepper, remove core and seeds, and cut into fine strips.

Place the canned tomatoes in a large saucepan and add all the other ingredients. Bring to the boil and skim any sediment if necessary. Cover and simmer for about 20 minutes or until all vegetables are tender. If there is too much liquid remaining, reduce this by boiling briskly for a few minutes with the lid removed.

*N.B. Ratatouille can be used as a main course if accompanied by a chicken joint or 8 oz (225 g) white fish (cooked weight).*

## Recipe 28
### Grilled Grapefruit

*(Serves 2)*

1 grapefruit
2 tablespoons sweet sherry
2 teaspoons brown sugar

Cut grapefruit in half. Remove core and membranes between segments with a grapefruit knife. Pour the sherry over the flesh, and sprinkle on the brown sugar. Place under a hot grill until sugar is glazed.

Serve hot.

## Recipe 29
## Stir-fried Chicken and Vegetables

(*Serves 1*)

4 oz (100 g) chicken (no skin), coarsely sliced
15 oz (425 g) tin bean sprouts, drained
3 sticks of celery, washed and finely sliced
2 carrots, peeled and coarsely grated
1 Spanish onion, peeled and finely sliced
3 oz (75 g) mushrooms, washed and sliced
1 oz (25 g) dry weight brown rice

Partly cook sliced chicken in a non-stick frying pan or wok until it changes colour. Add the prepared vegetables, a little at a time, until all ingredients are lightly cooked.

Serve with boiled brown rice.

## Recipe 30
## Haddock Florentine

(*Serves 1*)

10 oz (275 g) haddock or cod
lemon juice
1 lb (450 g) cooked spinach, chopped
*or* 10 oz (275 g) frozen spinach, thawed and drained

5 oz (150 g) natural yogurt
salt
freshly ground black pepper
1 lemon for garnish

Place the yogurt in a saucepan and add the chopped spinach. Heat gently, stirring continuously. Do not boil as the yogurt will curdle. Add salt and black pepper to taste.

Place the fish, sprinkled with lemon juice, in a microwave and cook on full power for 8 minutes. Alternatively, grill on tin foil, keeping it moist with lemon juice, or steam in skimmed milk.

Place the spinach mixture on a hot serving dish and arrange the fish on top.

Serve with wedges of lemon.

*NB. Smoked haddock can be used for this dish if preferred.*

## Recipe 31
## Chicken Veronique

(*Serves 4*)

1 whole chicken (4 lb) [1.6 kg]
½ pint (250 ml) chicken stock
2 fl oz (50 ml) skimmed milk
2 tablespoons cornflour
8 oz (225 g) green grapes
4 sprigs tarragon or 1 teaspoon ground tarragon
salt and freshly ground black pepper

Wash the chicken and season with tarragon, salt and pepper inside as this will penetrate the flesh.

Place chicken on a rack to keep it away from the fat as it drips away during cooking. Cover with tin foil and cook for 1½ hours at 200°C, 400°F, or Gas Mark 6. Remove foil 30 minutes from end of cooking time.

The grapes must now be peeled and deseeded. If they are difficult to peel, scald them with boiling water for 10 seconds and then drain and place in cold water for 10 seconds. The skin can then be removed easily. Remove the pips. Place the peeled, pipped grapes in an airtight container while you make the sauce.

*Sauce*

Chicken stock should ideally be made from the giblets which are boiled with an onion, bay leaf and peppercorns in water for 30 minutes, allowed to cool, and then drained of any fat after it has set. A chicken stock cube added to this liquid will strengthen the flavour. If there are no giblets available, make up ½ pint (250 ml) of stock with two stock cubes.

Mix the cornflour with the skimmed milk and carefully add to the stock liquid, stirring continuously. Heat gently and bring to the boil, continuing to stir all the time.

When everything is prepared add the grapes to the chicken sauce which will be light in colour.

Serve chicken either whole or in small joints which can be placed on a bed of sliced onions and potatoes cooked in chicken stock. If the chicken is served whole, serve the sauce separately in a boat. If it is served already jointed, pour the sauce over the completed dish.

## Recipe 32
### Lyonnaise Potatoes

(*Serves 2–4*)

1 lb (450 g) potatoes scrubbed but not peeled
2 large Spanish onions
¼–½ pint (125–250 ml) skimmed milk
garlic granules
chopped parsley

Slice the onions and potatoes. Place in layers in a casserole dish, sprinkling a few garlic granules between layers. Pour over enough skimmed milk almost to reach the top layer of the vegetables. Cover and cook in a moderately hot oven (200°C, 400°F, Gas Mark 6) for ¾ - 1 hour or until tender.
Garnish with chopped parsley.

## Recipe 33
### Tandoori Chicken

(*Serves 4*)

4 × 6 oz (175 g) chicken breasts, skin removed
1 clove garlic, peeled and crushed
1½ tablespoons tandoori powder
½ pint (250 ml) plain unsweetened yogurt

Make incisions in the flesh of the chicken. Mix the tandoori powder and yogurt together, and with a pastry brush work the mixture into the incisions in the chicken. Mix the crushed garlic into the remaining mixture and paint this all over the chicken joints. Place in a covered dish and leave to marinate for at least 4 hours, preferably longer, turning occasionally.

Pre-heat your grill at medium heat; place the joints on the baking rack, and cook for approximately 25 minutes, turning frequently and painting the remaining marinade at frequent intervals to avoid burning.

Serve with green salad and boiled brown rice.

## Recipe 34
## Shepherds' Pie

(*Serves 4*)

1 lb (450 g) minced beef
½ pint (250 ml) water
1 large onion, finely chopped
1 teaspoon mixed herbs
1 teaspoon yeast, or beef and vegetable extract, e.g. Marmite or Bovril
1 teaspoon gravy powder
1½ lbs (700 g) potatoes, peeled
salt and freshly ground black pepper

Boil mince and water in a saucepan for 5 minutes. Drain mince and place in a covered container until required. Meanwhile, place the drained liquid in the refrigerator. This will cause any fat to rise to the top and set hard so that it can be removed and discarded.

Replace the skimmed liquid in a saucepan. Add the mince, chopped onion, herbs, salt and pepper, and the yeast or beef extract. Mix gravy powder with a little water and add to the meat mixture. Bring to the boil, stirring continually, and leave to simmer for a further 10 minutes.

Boil the potatoes until soft, then remove most of the water, but not all of it as the potatoes need to be quite wet for mashing. Mash the potatoes and season well, adding a little skimmed milk if necessary to make a soft consistency.

Place the mince in an oval ovenproof dish and cover with the mashed potatoes. Place under a preheated grill to brown the top or in a preheated oven for 10 minutes.

Serve with unlimited vegetables.

## Recipe 35
## Fish Curry

(*Serves 2*)

2 pieces frozen haddock
15 oz (425 g) tin tomatoes
bay leaf
1 eating apple, cored and chopped small
2 teaspoons Branston pickle
1 teaspoon tomato purée
1 medium onion, finely chopped
1 tablespoon curry powder

Place all the ingredients except the fish in a saucepan, and bring to the boil. Put a lid on the saucepan and cook slowly for about 1 hour, stirring occasionally. Approximately 20 minutes before the end of cooking time, add the fish to the saucepan.

If the mixture is too thin, remove the lid and cook on a slightly higher heat until the sauce reduces and thickens towards the end of cooking time.

Serve on a bed of boiled brown rice.

# Recipe 36
## Steak Surprise

(*Serves 1*)

4 oz (100 g) rump or sirloin steak
1 clove crushed garlic *or* a sprinkle of dried minced garlic/garlic granules
1 pinch mixed herbs

Sprinkle garlic and herbs on to meat and work into the flesh on both sides with a steak hammer or a fork. Leave for several hours for the flavour to penetrate the flesh. Heat the grill at full temperature for 5 minutes until it is really hot.

Place steak on grill pan and turn after 1 minute to seal in the juices. Lower the grill rack and continue to cook to your liking – rare, medium rare, etc.

Serve with jacket potato, mushrooms cooked in stock, peas and salad.


# Recipe 37
## Barbecue Sauce

(*Serves 2*)

1 teaspoon plain flour
1/3 pint (167 ml) potato stock
1 tablespoon soy sauce
dash Worcester sauce
salt and pepper
small tin tomatoes

Skim off all fat from grill pan after cooking meat or poultry, leaving any sediment. To this fat free sediment, add the flour and a tablespoon of the stock. Stir well and cook very gently for 2–3 minutes.

Draw aside and blend in potato stock, sauces and seasonings. Return to heat and stir until boiling. Add the tinned tomatoes finely chopped (scissor snipped). Simmer for a minute or until it takes on a creamy consistency.

This sauce goes well with kebabs and grilled or baked chicken.

## Recipe 38
## Scous *or* Scaws (traditional hotpot)

(*Serves 4*)

1 lb (450 g) rump/stewing/shin beef, cut up to one-inch (2.5 cm) cubes
2 pints (1 litre) water
sea salt and ground pepper to taste

This is best prepared the night before.

Place the meat in a casserole; add water and boil for 1–1½ hours. Take off the heat and leave to cool. When cooled, skim off all fat.

Bring to the boil again, and add:

2 tablespoons Worcester sauce
1 teaspoon dried mushrooms
1½–2 lbs (700–900 g) potatoes, diced
1 carrot, diced
1 turnip, diced
1 parsnip, diced
1 onion, diced or sliced into rings
1 or 2 leeks sliced into rings
1 swede, diced

1 vegetable stock cube
1 beef stock cube
1 squeeze tomato purée (about ½ inch–¾ inch)
[1.2–1.9 cm]
6 oz (175 g) peas (if frozen add to the pot 1½ hours before serving)

Simmer for about 6–8 hours (or slow cook for 12 hours) and check seasoning occasionally. Top up occasionally with boiling water.

Serve with red cabbage and triangles of bread (no butter).

## Recipe 39
## Spaghetti Bolognese

(*Serves 2*)

4 oz (100 g) chicken livers (or lamb's liver)
½ pint (250 ml) beef stock
1 medium-sized onion, sliced
1 clove garlic, chopped, or ½ teaspoon dried minced garlic
3 teaspoons tomato purée
1 rounded dessertspoon plain flour
1 tablespoon sweet sherry
salt and freshly ground black pepper
spaghetti

Sauté the livers in a non-stick frying pan until they have changed colour. Remove from pan.

Add a little stock to the pan. Add the onion, tomato purée and garlic. Stir in the flour and mix well. Add the remaining stock and the sherry and continue to stir until boiling. Simmer for 10 minutes and add the livers, coarsely chopped.

Continue to simmer until sauce becomes thick, approximately 10 minutes. Season to taste and serve on a bed of boiled spaghetti.

*N.B. The spaghetti must be an egg-free variety and boiled in water. Add no butter.*

## Recipe 40
## Barbecued Chicken Kebabs

(*Serves 2*)

*For kebabs*

2 large chicken joints, preferably breasts, boned and with all fat and skin removed
2 medium-sized onions, peeled and cut into quarters
1 green pepper/1 red pepper with core and seeds removed, cut into bite-sized squares
6 oz (175 g) mushrooms, washed but left whole
8 bay leaves

*For barbecue sauce*

2 tablespoons tomato ketchup
2 tablespoons brown sauce
2 tablespoons mushroom sauce (optional)
2 tablespoons wine vinegar

Cut the chicken flesh into cubes large enough to be placed on a skewer. Thread on to two skewers alternately with bite-sized pieces of onion, green and red peppers and mushrooms, placing a bay leaf on the skewer at intervals to add flavour.

Mix all the sauce ingredients together and brush on to the skewers filled with the chicken and vegetables. If you have time, brush the sauce on a couple of hours before cooking, as this will add greatly to the flavour.

Place the skewers under the grill and cook under a moderate heat, turning frequently to avoid burning. Continue to baste with the sauce mixture to maintain the moisture. Use no fat.

Serve on a bed of boiled brown rice and grilled fresh tomatoes.

## Recipe 41
## Chicken or Prawn Chop Suey

(*Serves 1*)

1 chicken joint, skinned and boned, *or* 4 oz (100g) prawns
1 tablespoon vegetable stock
1 large carrot, peeled and coarsely grated
2 sticks celery, finely chopped
1 large onion, finely sliced
1 green pepper, deseeded and sliced
15 oz (425 g) tin bean sprouts, drained
salt and pepper to taste
soy sauce

Coarsely slice the chicken, add to the vegetable stock and cook in a large non-stick frying pan or wok on a moderate heat until it changes colour. Add grated carrot, sliced onion and celery, and stir fry.

Add the sliced green pepper and bean sprouts and continue to cook until thoroughly hot. Season to taste.

Serve on a bed of boiled brown rice with soy sauce.

# Recipe 42
## Vegetable Chop Suey

(*Serves 1*)

1 large carrot, peeled and coarsely grated
3 sticks celery, finely chopped
1 large onion, finely chopped
15 oz (425 g) tin bean sprouts, drained
1 green pepper, deseeded and sliced
1 tablespoon vegetable stock
salt and pepper to taste
soy sauce

Pour a little stock into a non-stick frying pan or wok. Add all ingredients except bean sprouts, and stir fry. When the vegetables are hot and partly cooked add the drained bean sprouts. Continue to cook for 5 minutes until hot.

Serve on a bed of boiled brown rice, with soy sauce.

# Recipe 43
## Chicken Curry

(*Serves 2*)

2 chicken joints with all fat and skin removed
15 oz (425 g) tin tomatoes
bay leaf
1 eating apple, cored and chopped small
2 teaspoons Branston pickle
1 teaspoon tomato purée
1 medium onion, finely chopped
1 tablespoon curry powder

Place the chicken joints and all the ingredients in

a saucepan and bring to the boil. Put a lid on the saucepan and cook slowly for about one hour, stirring occasionally and making sure the chicken joints are turned every 15 minutes or so. If the mixture is too thin, remove the lid and cook on a slightly higher heat until the sauce reduces and thickens.

Serve on a bed of boiled brown rice.

## Recipe 44
## Fish Pie

(*Serves 4*)

1½ lbs (700 g) cod
1½ lbs (700 g) potatoes
salt and pepper
2 oz (50 g) Shape or Tendale Cheddar optional, for maintenance dieters only

Bake, steam or microwave the fish but do not overcook. Season well.

Boil the potatoes until well done and mash with a little water to make a soft consistency. Season well.

Place fish in an ovenproof dish. Flake the flesh, remove the skin, and distribute the fish evenly across the base of the dish. Sprinkle the grated cheese at this point if you are on the maintenance diet.

Cover the fish completely with the mashed potatoes and smooth over with a fork. Sprinkle a little cheese on the top if desired.

If the ingredients are still hot just place under a hot grill for a few minutes to brown the top.

Alternatively the pie can be made well in advance and then warmed through in a preheated moderate oven (180°C, 350°F, Gas Mark 4) for 20 minutes, or microwaved on *high* for 5 minutes.

## Recipe 45
## Chinese Chicken

(*Serves 1*)

6 oz (175 g) chicken, skinned and cut into strips
½ Spanish onion, coarsely chopped
1 teaspoon Schwartz Chinese seasoning
6 tablespoons water
2 tablespoons soy sauce
2 tablespoons lemon juice
4 oz (100 g) cut green beans
3 oz (75 g) cucumber, cut into 2-inch (5 cm) lengths
½ red pepper, deseeded and cut into strips
4 oz (100 g) button mushrooms, cut in half
4 oz (100 g) beansprouts
3 oz (75 g) sweetcorn

Dry fry the chicken and onion in a non-stick frying pan or wok for about 5 minutes. Stir in the Chinese seasoning, water, soy sauce and lemon juice. Bring to the boil. Reduce the heat and add all remaining vegetables. Stir thoroughly and cook for approximately 5 minutes.

Serve piping hot on to a hot plate.

# Recipe 46
## Fish Risotto

*(Serves 4)*

3 frozen haddock fillets
4 tablespoons brown rice
1 chopped onion
oregano
1 glass white wine
8 oz (225 g) tin tomatoes
2 oz (50 g) mushrooms, sliced
2 oz (50 g) frozen peas
salt and black pepper
1 oz (25 g) Shape or Tendale Cheddar cheese (grated)
– optional, for maintenance dieters only

Poach the fish in the water until it is cooked. Remove the skin and break the flesh into chunks.

Meanwhile, cook rice in salted water, adding the chopped onion as soon as rice is simmering.

When the rice is half-cooked, add the oregano, pepper, mushrooms and tomatoes. Next add the glass of wine and the frozen peas.

Add the fish when almost all the liquid has evaporated.

If you are on the maintenance diet, you can sprinkle the risotto with cheese before serving.

For special occasions, you could add green peppers or prawns.

## Recipe 47
## Stuffed Marrow

(*Serves 4*)

1 medium-sized marrow, skinned, cut lengthways and seeded

*Stuffing*

assorted vegetables, chopped
2 teaspoons chopped fresh rosemary or 1 teaspoon dried rosemary
2 tablespoons tomato purée
1 oz (25 g) chopped onion
salt and freshly ground black pepper
4 oz (100 g) long grain brown rice
2 cloves garlic, peeled and crushed

Cook the vegetables, onion, garlic, tomato purée and rosemary in a little water seasoned with salt and pepper. Simmer until tender. Leave this mixture for the flavour to develop overnight.

Cook the rice in a saucepan of boiling salted water until tender. Mix the rice with the vegetable mixture and spoon into the marrow halves.

Wrap the stuffed marrow in foil and bake in the oven at 200°C, 400°F, or Gas Mark 6 for 1 hour.

## Recipe 48
## Vegetable Bake

(*Serves 1*)

Selection of vegetables, e.g. carrots, parsnips, peas, cabbage, leeks, onions
6 oz (175 g) potato, cooked

4 oz (100 g) mushrooms
3 tablespoons packet stuffing mix
1 teaspoon mixed herbs
cup of breadcrumbs – preferably wholemeal
½ pint (250 ml) vegetable stock

Cook the vegetables, chop them, and place in layers in a large ovenproof dish. Sprinkle the mixed herbs and stuffing mix between layers.

Slice the mushrooms and place over the other vegetables. Then, slice the pre-cooked potato, carefully lay across the top of the dish and sprinkle with the breadcrumbs. Carefully pour over the vegetable stock to moisten the contents of the dish.

Bake in a moderate oven (180°C, 350°F, Gas Mark 4) for 20 minutes until piping hot. Alternatively, reheat in a microwave on medium for 7 minutes and place under a hot grill for 5 minutes to crisp the top.

## Recipe 49
## Vegetarian Goulash

(*Serves 2*)

3 oz (75 g) soya chunks
1 large onion, chopped
3 oz (75 g) carrots, sliced
3 oz (75 g) potato cut into small chunks
15 oz (425 g) tin tomatoes
½ pint (250 ml) vegetable stock
1 red pepper, deseeded and chopped
2 bay leaves
2 teaspoons paprika
3 tablespoons natural yogurt
salt and black pepper to taste

Soak the soya chunks in 2 cupfuls of boiling water for 10 minutes and drain.

Place all the ingredients except the yogurt in a saucepan. Bring to the boil, cover and simmer for about 1 hour. Stir in the yogurt and season to taste.

Serve with boiled brown rice or wholewheat pasta.

## Recipe 50
## Vegetarian Shepherds' Pie

(*Serves 4*)

3 oz (75 g) dry weight soya savoury mince
1 large onion, finely sliced
15 oz (425 g) tin tomatoes, chopped finely
1 teaspoon mixed herbs
1 teaspoon yeast extract
4 fl oz (100 ml) vegetable stock
1 tablespoon gravy powder mixed in a little water
1½ lbs (700 g) cooked potatoes, mashed (with water only)
salt and freshly ground black pepper

Add soya savoury mince to 2 cups of boiling water and leave to soak for 10 minutes. Drain.

Place the soya mince, onion, tomatoes, herbs, seasoning, yeast extract and vegetable stock in a saucepan. Bring to the boil and simmer for 20 minutes. Add the gravy powder mixed with water and stir until mixture thickens. Simmer uncovered for a further 5 minutes.

Place the mince mixture in an oval ovenproof dish and cover with the mashed potatoes. Place under a preheated grill to brown the top, or in a preheated oven (160°C, 325°F, Gas Mark 3) for 10 minutes.

Serve with unlimited vegetables.

## Recipe 51
## Vegetable Curry

(*Serves 4*)

3 oz (75 g) dry weight soya chunks
15 oz (425 g) tin tomatoes
bay leaf
1 eating apple, chopped
2 teaspoons Branston pickle
1 teaspoon tomato purée
1 medium onion, chopped
1 tablespoon curry powder

Soak the soya chunks in 2 cups of boiling water for 10 minutes. Drain.

Place the soya chunks and all other ingredients in a saucepan and bring to the boil. Cover the saucepan and simmer for about 1 hour, stirring occasionally. If the mixture is too thin, remove the lid and cook on a slightly higher heat until the sauce reduces and thickens.

Serve on a bed of boiled brown rice.

## Recipe 52
## Vegetarian Chilli con Carne

(*Serves 4*)

3 oz (75 g) dry weight soya savoury mince
15 oz (425 g) tin tomatoes

2 bay leaves
1 large onion, chopped
1 teaspoon yeast extract
15 oz (425 g) tin red kidney beans
1 teaspoon chilli powder (adjust this ingredient to your individual taste)
1 teaspoon garlic granules, optional

Add 2 cups of boiling water to soya mince and leave to soak for 10 minutes.

Place all ingredients in a saucepan, cover and cook for 30 minutes. Remove lid and continue cooking until it reaches a fairly thick consistency.

Serve with boiled brown rice.

## Recipe 53
## Vegetable Chilli

(*Serves 4*)

15 oz (425 g) tin tomatoes
bay leaf
1 eating apple, chopped
2 teaspoons Branston pickle
1 teaspoon tomato purée
1 medium onion, chopped
4 oz (100 g) broad beans
4 oz (100 g) peas
4 oz (100 g) carrots, peeled and chopped
4 oz (100 g) potatoes, peeled and chopped
8 oz (225 g) tin baked beans or red kidney beans
1 teaspoon chilli powder ⎫ adjust seasoning
3 chillis ⎬ to individual
1 teaspoon garlic granules ⎭ taste
4 fl oz (100 ml) vegetable stock

Place all ingredients in a saucepan and cover.

Simmer for 1 hour, stirring occasionally. Remove lid and continue to cook until of a thick consistency, raising the heat if necessary to reduce the liquid.

Serve on a bed of boiled brown rice.

## Recipe 54
## Vegetarian Spaghetti Bolognese

*(Serves 4)*

3 oz (75 g) dry weight soya mince
3 oz (75 g) mushrooms
15 oz (425 g) tin tomatoes
1 teaspoon yeast extract
½ green pepper, deseeded and finely chopped
1 teaspoon oregano
2 cloves garlic, chopped
1 tablespoon gravy powder
fat free spaghetti

Pre-soak the soya mince in 2 cups of boiling water and leave to stand for 10 minutes. Drain.

Place soya mince, mushrooms, tomatoes, pepper, yeast extract, oregano and garlic in a saucepan; cover and simmer for 20 minutes. Mix gravy powder with a little cold water and mix into the sauce mixture.

Boil spaghetti for 10–20 minutes until tender. Drain and place in a serving dish. Pour sauce on top.

## Recipe 55
## Mushroom Stroganoff

(*Serves 4*)

3 oz (75 g) soya savoury chunks
1 large onion, finely chopped
8 oz (251 g) button mushrooms
¼ pint (125 ml) vegetable stock
¼ pint (125 ml) skimmed milk
1 teaspoon mixed herbs
2 dessertspoons cornflour
3 oz (75 g) natural yogurt
salt and freshly ground black pepper

Pre-soak the savoury chunks in 2 cups of boiling water for 10 minutes. Drain.

Place all ingredients except cornflour and yogurt in a large saucepan and heat slowly. Mix the cornflour with a little water and add to mixture when it is almost boiling, stirring continually to make a smooth sauce. Continue to cook on a gentle heat for a further 10 minutes. Stir in the yogurt and taste for seasoning.

Serve with boiled brown rice and unlimited vegetables.

## Recipe 56
## Bean Salad

(*Serves 2*)

8 oz (225 g) tin red kidney beans
8 oz (225 g) tin chick peas
8 oz (225 g) tin butter beans
8 oz (225 g) tin cut green beans

1 Spanish onion, peeled and chopped
4 tomatoes, chopped
cucumber, cut into small pieces
3 sticks celery, washed and finely sliced
3 oz (75 g) sultanas
5 oz (150 g) natural yogurt
freshly ground black pepper
salt

Drain the beans and chick peas. Mix with chopped vegetables and sultanas. Mix in the yogurt, and season to taste.

Serve as a meal in itself or with other salad vegetables.

## Recipe 57
## Hummus with Crudités

(*Serves 2*)

*Hummus*
4 oz (100 g) chick peas, pre-soaked in cold water overnight
7 tablespoons skimmed milk in addition to allowance
1 tablespoon lemon juice
½ teaspoon mild chilli powder
¼ teaspoon garlic granules
¼ teaspoon ground white pepper
salt
2 tablespoons natural yogurt

*Crudités*
red pepper
cucumber  } all cut into sticks
celery
cauliflower florets – for dipping

Drain the chick peas and place in a saucepan. Cover with fresh water and bring to the boil. Reduce the heat, cover and simmer gently for 2–2¼ hours until chick peas are soft. Drain.

Place chick peas, skimmed milk and lemon juice in a food processor or liquidizer and blend on high speed until mixture is pale and smooth. Stir in the chilli powder, garlic granules, white pepper, salt and yogurt.

Spoon into a serving dish and chill before serving.

Serve with raw vegetable sticks, and cauliflower florets.

## Recipe 58
## Spiced Bean Casserole

(*Serves 2*)

2 oz (50 g) chopped onion
¾ teaspoon mild chilli powder
8 oz (225 g) tin tomatoes
½ tablespoon tomato purée
1 oz (25 g) wholemeal flour
¼ pint (125 ml) beef flavour stock
¼ teaspoon garlic granules
pinch of salt
4 oz (100 g) sliced courgettes
6 oz (175 g) sliced red and green peppers
8 oz (225 g) tin red kidney beans, washed and drained
8 oz (225 g) tin haricot beans
4 oz (100 g) sweetcorn

Dry fry the onion in a non-stick frying pan until soft. Add tinned tomatoes and mild chilli powder, tomato purée and wholemeal flour and mix well.

Gradually add the beef flavoured stock together with the garlic granules, salt, sliced courgettes and peppers. Add the drained beans and sweetcorn and bring to the boil. Cover and simmer for 10–12 minutes or until the vegetables are tender.

Serve with mashed potatoes or boiled rice.

## Recipe 59
## Vegetable Kebabs

(*Serves 2*)

1 green pepper, deseeded and chopped into ¾ in (2 cm) squares
1 red pepper, deseeded and chopped into ¾ in (2 cm) squares
1 large Spanish onion, peeled and cut into large pieces (or 6 oz [175 g] small button onions, peeled)
8 oz (225 g) button mushrooms, washed
4 courgettes, coarsely sliced
1 lb (450 g) average sized fresh tomatoes sliced across sideways
1 teaspoon thyme
cayenne pepper
tin foil
2 oz (50 g) Edam or low fat Cheddar cheese (for maintenance dieters only)

Preheat oven to 180°C, 350°F, or Gas Mark 4.

Thread vegetable pieces alternatively on four skewers to make four kebabs.

Cover a baking sheet with foil and place the kebabs on the foil, sprinkling each kebab with thyme. Wrap the foil around the kebabs to make a parcel and cook for 35 minutes.

Remove from oven. Place on a bed of hot sweetcorn and boiled rice and sprinkle with cayenne pepper to taste. Replace in the oven for 1 minute.

*For maintenance programme only:* Grated Edam or low fat Cheddar cheese may be sprinkled on to the kebabs at the end of first 35 minutes cooking. Then place serving dish under a preheated grill for 2 minutes to melt cheese.

## Recipe 60
## Vegetable Casserole

*(Serves 1)*

Selection of vegetables (approx 1 lb [450 g] in total)
4 oz (100 g) lentils (pre-soaked)
1 teaspoon paprika
1 pinch garlic granules
salt and freshly ground black pepper
½ pint (250 ml) water or vegetable stock

Place chopped vegetables and lentils in a casserole and sprinkle with the paprika and garlic granules. Add salt, pepper and stock and cover.

Place in a moderate oven (180°C, 350°F, Gas Mark 4) and cook for approximately 1 hour or until vegetables are tender.

Alternatively, this dish could be cooked in a microwave for 20–25 minutes on full power, but use only 3 fl oz (75 ml) water.

## Recipe 61
## Three Bean Salad

*(Serves 4)*

15 oz (425 g) tin red kidney beans, drained and washed
15 oz (425 g) tin haricot beans, drained and washed
8 oz (225 g) tin butter beans, drained and washed
cucumber, finely chopped
tomatoes, finely chopped
4 sticks celery, finely sliced
spring onions, finely sliced
red and green peppers, finely chopped
1 Spanish onion, finely chopped
sprinkling of oregano and sage
salt and freshly ground black pepper

Mix all ingredients together in a large bowl. Serve chilled with French bread or garlic bread if you are on the Maintenance Programme.

## Recipe 62
## Stuffed Peppers

*(Serves 1)*

2 peppers, red or green
1 oz (25 g) [uncooked weight] brown rice
1 teaspoon mixed herbs
1 teaspoon sweetcorn
1 teaspoon peas
1 teaspoon mushrooms, chopped
½ medium onion, chopped
salt and freshly ground black pepper

Wash the peppers; remove the tops and scoop out the seeds.

Boil the rice with the herbs until the rice is tender. Mix rice and other vegetables together and pile into the peppers. Place on a baking tray in a moderate oven (160°C, 325°F, Gas Mark 3), for 20 minutes.

Serve with other vegetables if desired.

## Recipe 63
## Black Eye Bean Casserole

(*Serves 2*)

2 oz (50 g) black eye beans
2 oz (50 g) diced onion
6 oz (175 g) sliced mushrooms
4 oz (100 g) celery, cut into thin strips
3 oz (75 g) carrots, cut into thin strips
2 oz (50 g) water chestnuts, thinly sliced
½ teaspoon chilli powder
½ teaspoon grated fresh ginger or ½ teaspoon ground ginger
1 clove garlic
½ oz (12 g) cornflour
1 tablespoon soy sauce
¼ pint (125 ml) vegetable stock
freshly ground black pepper

Cook the black eye beans in plenty of water for 30–35 minutes, by bringing to the boil and then simmering in a covered pan.

Gently heat the vegetables, chilli, ginger and garlic in a little stock for 10 minutes. Mix the cornflour and soy sauce with a little stock and then stir in remainder of the stock. Add this mixture to the vegetables and then add the drained beans. Simmer for 8–10 minutes and season to taste.

Serve on a bed of boiled brown rice.

## Recipe 64
## Chick Pea and Fennel Casserole

(*Serves* 2)

3 oz (75 g) cooked chick peas
1 oz (25 g) Bulgar wheat
1 clove garlic, crushed
6 oz (175 g) diced celery
6 oz (175 g) whole green beans, chopped
½ pint (250 ml) vegetable stock
2 tablespoons soy sauce
2 tablespoons chopped mint, preferably fresh
1 dessertspoon crushed fennel seeds
salt and freshly ground black pepper

Cook the chick peas, wheat, celery, fennel and garlic gently in a little stock for about 5 minutes. Add the remaining ingredients, excluding the mint.

Simmer for 20 minutes and serve with fresh mint and unlimited vegetables.

## Recipe 65
## Fruit Sundae

(*Serves* 2)

½ lb (225 g) fruit (blackberries or raspberries or strawberries or a mixture)
6 drops liquid artificial sweetener *or*
1 tablespoon granulated artificial sweetener
5 oz (150 g) plain yogurt
1 egg white

Stir the fruit, sweetener and yogurt together thoroughly.

Whisk the egg white until stiff and fold in the fruit mixture.

Spoon into serving glasses. Top with angelica and vermouth if desired.

## Recipe 66
## Low Fat Custard

(*Serves 2*)

½ pint (250 ml) skimmed milk
8 saccharin tablets or 15 drops of liquid sweetener
1 tablespoon custard powder

Heat most of the milk in a non-stick saucepan. Mix the remainder of the milk with the custard powder and add slowly to the heated milk, stirring continuously.

Add saccharin tablets and continue to stir until boiling. Simmer for approximately 5 minutes.

## Recipe 67
## Apple and Blackcurrant Whip

(*Serves 4*)

1 lb (450 g) cooking apples
2 fl oz (50 ml) water
Saccharin or liquid sweetener to taste
2 egg whites
2 tablespoons low calorie blackcurrant jam or 4 oz (100 g) fresh or frozen blackcurrants

Peel, core and slice apples and cook with the water until it becomes a thick pulp. Add sweetener. Set aside to cool.

Whisk egg whites until stiff and fold gently into cooled apple purée.

Pile into individual sundae dishes or a medium-sized serving dish. Swirl jam or blackcurrant fruit on the top to give a marble/ripple effect.

## Recipe 68
## Pineapple and Orange Sorbet

*(Serves 6)*

Small tin of crushed pineapples in natural juice
1 orange, peeled and chopped
2 egg whites
liquid sweetener
8 fl oz (200 ml) fresh orange juice

Crush pineapple well and mix with chopped orange, and orange juice. Place in a plastic container in your freezer or the freezer compartment in your refrigerator. Freeze until half frozen.

Whisk egg whites until stiff. Turn out half-frozen mixture into a mixing bowl and fold in whisked egg whites.

Return mixture to freezer until firm.

## Recipe 69
## Raspberry Mousse

*(Serves 4)*

8 oz (225 g) fresh or frozen raspberries (or 7 oz
[200 g] tin raspberries in natural juice)
4 oz (100 g) natural apple juice
liquid sweetener, approximately 15 drops

1 teaspoon gelatine
2 egg whites
1 teaspoon raspberry yogurt
12 fresh raspberries to decorate

Place raspberries and apple juice in a liquidizer and blend until smooth. Strain through a sieve into a basin. Add liquid sweetener to taste.

Dissolve gelatine in 3 teaspoons of water in a cup over very hot water. Add to raspberry purée and stir well.

Whisk egg whites until they form peaks. Fold into purée.

Pour mixture into tall sundae glasses or a serving dish. Decorate with a teaspoon of raspberry yogurt and fresh raspberries.

## Recipe 70
## Pears in Red Wine

(*Serves 4*)

6 ripe pears, peeled but left whole
2 oz (50 g) brown sugar
2 wine glasses of red wine
2 fl oz (50 ml) water
½ level teaspoon cinnamon or ground ginger

*To microwave*
Combine wine, water, sugar and spice in a glass jug and microwave on *high* for approximately 4 minutes or until boiling.

Place the pears in a deep soufflé dish, pour wine sauce over them and cover with cling film. Microwave on *high* for approximately 5 minutes or until just tender but retaining their shape.

*To cook on stove*

Combine wine, water, sugar and spice in a large saucepan, and bring to the boil. Add the pears to the pan and simmer for 10–15 minutes, turning the pears carefully from time to time to ensure even colouring.

Serve hot or cold. Maintenance Dieters may serve with Shape Single or ice cream.

## Recipe 71
## Pineapple in Kirsch

(*Serves 4*)

1 fresh pineapple
Liqueur/sherry glass of Kirsch

Remove skin and core from the pineapple and slice into rings.

Sprinkle the Kirsch over the fruit and place in a refrigerator for at least 12 hours to marinate. Keep turning the fruit to ensure even flavouring.

Maintenance Dieters may serve with Shape Single or ice cream if desired.

## Recipe 72
## Oranges in Cointreau

(*Serves 4*)

6 oranges – medium size
wine glass of medium to sweet white wine *or* fresh orange juice
sherry glass of Cointreau or Grand Marnier liqueur
liquid artificial sweetener if desired

Heat white wine or orange juice and liqueur in a saucepan and add sweetener to taste. Allow to cool.

Carefully peel the oranges with a sharp knife to remove all pith. This can be done by slicing the peel across the top of the orange and then using the flat end of the orange as a base. Cut strips of peel away from the top downwards with a very sharp knife so that the orange is completely free from the white membranes of the peel. Squeeze the peel to extract any juice and pour this into the wine mixture.

Slice the oranges across to form round slices of equal size and place in the liquid when cool.

Allow to stand in a refrigerator for at least 12 hours.

Serve in glass dishes.

## Recipe 73
## Diet Rice Pudding

(*Serves 4*)

1 pint (500 ml) low fat skimmed milk
1 oz (25 g) pudding rice
artificial sweetener to taste (approximately 20 saccharin tablets or 20 drops of liquid sweetener)
pinch of nutmeg (optional)

Place all ingredients except nutmeg in an ovenproof dish. Sprinkle the nutmeg over the top. Cook in the oven for 2–2½ hours at 150°C, 300°F, or Gas Mark 2. If the pudding is still sloppy 30–40 minutes before it is to be eaten, raise the oven temperature to 160°C, 325°F, Gas Mark 3.

Serve hot or cold. If you intend to serve cold,

remove from oven while still very moist as it will become stiffer and drier when cool.

## Recipe 74
## Fruit Sorbet

(*Serves 6*)

1 lb (450 g) fruit making ¼ pint (125 ml) fruit purée (preferably strong-flavoured fruit e.g. blackcurrants, blackberries, strawberries, raspberries or black cherries. Tinned fruit may be used but remove syrup before liquidizing.)
2 large egg whites
artificial sweetener to taste (if desired)

If fresh fruit is used, cook approximately 1 lb (450 g) of fruit in very little water together with a sweetening agent if desired. When the fruit is soft and the liquid well coloured either place the cooked fruit in a sieve and work the pulp with a wooden spoon until as much as possible of the fruit has passed through the mesh. Alternatively use liquidizer.

Allow to cool and place the purée in a metal or plastic container, cover with a lid and freeze until it begins to set. When a layer of purée approximately half an inch (1 cm) thick has frozen, remove the mixture from the freezer and stir it so that the mixture is a soft crystallized consistency.

Whisk the two egg whites until stiff and standing in peaks. Fold into the semi-frozen purée to give a marbled effect. Immediately return the mixture to the freezer and freeze until firm.

Serve straight from the freezer.

# Recipe 75
## Pears in Meringue

(*Serves 6*)

6 ripe dessert pears, peeled but left whole
10 fl oz (300 ml) apple juice
3 egg whites
6 oz (175 g) caster sugar

Cook the pears in the apple juice until just tender but still firm. Cut a slice off the bottom of each pear to enable them to sit in a dish without falling over, and place in an ovenproof dish well spaced out.

Whisk the egg whites in a large and completely grease-free bowl, preferably with a balloon whisk or rotary beater, as these make more volume than an electric whisk.

When the egg whites are firm and stand in peaks, whisk in 1 tablespoon of the caster sugar for 1 minute. Fold in the remainder of the sugar with a metal spoon, cutting the egg whites rather than mixing them.

Place the egg white and sugar mixture into a large piping bag with a metal nozzle (any pattern) and pipe a pyramid around each pear starting from the base and working upwards. Place in a moderate oven (160°C, 325°F, Gas Mark 3), and cook until firm and golden.

Serve hot or cold. Maintenance Dieters may serve with Shape Single or ice cream if desired.

# Recipe 76
## Apple Gâteau

*(Serves 8: Maintenance Dieters only)*

*Makes one 8 in (20 cm) cake.*

3 eggs
4½ oz (112 g) caster sugar
3 oz (75 g) plain flour
pinch of salt
1 lb (450 g) eating apples, peeled, cored and sliced
grated rind and juice of 1 lemon
1 tablespoon apricot jam
artificial sweetener for apples if desired
1 teaspoon icing sugar

Very lightly grease an 8 in (20 cm) cake tin. Dust with caster sugar, then with flour. Shake out the excess.

Place the eggs and caster sugar in a mixing bowl and whisk with an electric whisk/mixer for 5 minutes at top speed. When thick and mousse-like, fold in the sifted flour and salt.

Pour into the prepared tin. Bake in the centre of a moderately hot oven (190°C, 375°F, Gas Mark 5) for 25 minutes or until golden brown and shrunk from the edges of the tin a little. Run a blunt knife around the inside of the tin and turn out the cake on to a wire rack to cool.

*For the filling:* Place the apple slices in a pan with the grated rind and juice of a lemon and the jam. Heat slowly. Add the artificial sweetener to taste if required. Cover and cook until the apples are just tender.

When the cake is cool, slice it across with a large knife to make two cakes. Spread the bottom half with the cooled apple filling and cover with the top half of the cake. Sprinkle with icing sugar on top.

## Recipe 77
## Garlic or Mint Yogurt Dip

5 oz (150 g) natural yogurt
1 clove garlic, finely chopped *or* 2 sprigs fresh mint, finely chopped
4 oz (100 g) plain cottage cheese

Mix all ingredients together. Serve in a small dish, accompanied by sticks of raw carrot, onion, peppers, cucumber and celery.

## Recipe 78
## Yogurt and Mint Dressing

5 oz (150 g) natural yogurt
1 teaspoon mint sauce
salt
freshly ground black pepper

Mix all the ingredients together and keep refrigerated. Chill before serving and serve on salads, jacket potatoes, etc.

## Recipe 79
## Jacket Potatoes

1 medium-sized potato per person
salt

Scrub well even-sized potatoes and make a single cut along the top. Roll them in salt and bake in the oven at 190°C, 375°F, Gas Mark 5 for one and a half hours (or until they give when pressed). Make cross-cuts on top of each potato and squeeze to enlarge cuts. Add filling of your choice. Serve at once.

*Alternative serving suggestion*
(*Serves 4: Maintenance Programme*)
Remove potato centres and place in a bowl, carefully preserving 'jackets'. Add 1 chopped onion, 2 oz (50 g) Shape or Tendale Cheddar flavour cheese, coarsely grated, salt and black pepper. Mix thoroughly and replace into potato skins. Return to the oven for 10 minutes to heat through before serving.

## Recipe 80
## Mashed Potatoes with Yogurt

Instead of using milk, cream or butter, mash the cooked potatoes with plain yogurt. Add a little ground pepper to make them even more delicious.

## Recipe 81
## Dry-roast Potatoes

Choose medium potatoes of even size. Peel and blanch them by putting into cold salted water and bringing to the boil.

Drain thoroughly, lightly scratch the surface of each potato with a fork, and sprinkle lightly with salt. Place in a non-stick baking tray, without fat, in a moderate oven (200°C, 400°F, Gas Mark 6) for about 1–1½ hours.

## Recipe 82
## Dry-roast Parsnips

Choose even-sized medium parsnips. Peel and blanch halved parsnips in cold salted water and bring to the boil.

Drain thoroughly and sprinkle lightly with salt. Place in a non-stick baking tray, without fat, in a moderate oven (200°C, 400°F, Gas Mark 6) for 30 minutes. Cook until soft in the centre when pierced with a fork.

## Recipe 83
## Garlic Spinach
(*Serves 4*)

1 lb (450 g) frozen chopped spinach
1 teaspoon minced garlic
1½ pints (750 ml) boiling water

Cook the spinach and garlic together for 5 minutes. Drain well, and serve.

## Recipe 84
## Stuffed Mushrooms

2 large mushrooms per person and two or three over
2 oz (50 ml) stock (vegetable or chicken)
1 teaspoon chopped onion

1 tablespoon fresh white breadcrumbs
salt and pepper
1 teaspoon parsley
pinch of dried mixed herbs

Cup mushrooms are best for this dish. Wash and peel them and cut across the stalks level with the caps as this helps prevent shrinkage.

Chop the trimmings along with the extra mushrooms. Cook for 1–2 minutes in the stock with the chopped onion. Add the crumbs, season, and add herbs.

Spread this mixture on to the mushrooms and arrange them on a baking sheet or in a fireproof dish. Bake for 12–15 minutes in a moderately hot oven (200°C, 400°F, Gas Mark 6). Serve immediately.

This dish is ideal to accompany any diet dinner menu.

## Recipe 85
## Garlic Sauce

8 oz (225 g) tin of tomatoes
3 cloves of garlic, peeled and finely chopped
1 teaspoon dried oregano or basil
salt
freshly ground black pepper

Place all the ingredients in a saucepan and simmer gently until piping hot. Serve as a sauce with steak or chicken.

## Recipe 86
## White Sauce

½ pint (250 ml) skimmed milk
1 dessertspoon cornflour
1 onion, peeled and sliced
6 peppercorns
1 bay leaf
salt and freshly ground black pepper

Heat all but 2 fl oz (50 ml) of the milk in a non-stick saucepan, adding the onion, peppercorns, bay leaf and seasoning. Heat gently and cover the pan. Simmer for 5 minutes. Turn off heat and leave milk mixture to stand, with the lid on, for a further 30 minutes or until ready to thicken and serve the sauce.

Mix remaining milk with cornflour and, when almost ready to serve, strain the milk, add the cornflour mixture and reheat slowly, stirring continuously, until it comes to the boil. If it begins to thicken too quickly, remove from heat and stir very fast to mix well. Cook for 3–4 minutes and serve immediately.

## Recipe 87
## Parsley Sauce

As White Sauce, but add chopped fresh parsley or dried parsley to taste during final cooking.

## Recipe 88
## Oil-free Vinaigrette Dressing

3 tablespoons white wine vinegar or cider vinegar
1 tablespoon lemon juice
½ teaspoon black pepper
½ teaspoon salt
1 teaspoon sugar
½ teaspoon French mustard
chopped herbs (thyme, marjoram, basil or parsley)

Mix all the ingredients together. Place in a sealed container and shake well. Taste and add more salt or sugar as desired.

## Recipe 89
## Bran Cake

1 mug bran
1 mug sultanas
½ mug sugar – white or brown
1 mug skimmed milk
1 mug self-raising flour

Soak the bran, sugar, milk and fruit together for at least 2 hours. Add flour and pour into a loaf tin. Bake at 180°C, 350°F, Gas Mark 4 for 1–1½ hours.
  Serve in slices. Dieters may consume an occasional slice as a treat!

## Recipe 90
## Hot Herb Loaf

(*Maintenance Programme*)

1 French loaf

4 oz (100 g) St Ivel 'Gold Lowest' very low fat spread
1 tablespoon mixed dried herbs
juice of ¼ lemon
black pepper
2 cloves of fresh garlic, crushed

Cream the very low fat spread with the herbs, lemon juice and pepper. If you like garlic, add a little now.

Cut the loaf into even, slanting slices about an inch thick. Spread each slice generously with low fat spread mixture and reshape loaf. Wrap in foil and bake for 10 minutes in a hot oven (220°C, 425°F, Gas Mark 7). Then reduce oven setting to 200°C, 400°F, Gas Mark 6 and open the foil so that the bread browns and crisps. This should take a further 5–8 minutes.

(If you wish to avoid the use of any fat, leave some slices without the spread, sprinkling them with herbs, lemon juice and garlic only.)

## Recipe 91
## Stilton Pears

*(Serves 4: Maintenance Programme)*

6 ripe pears
2 oz (50 g) Stilton cheese
8 oz (225 g) Shape soft low fat cheese
2 tablespoons skimmed milk
salt and pepper
juice of one lemon
1 oz flaked almonds, baked until brown

Peel pears and cut in half lengthways. Remove core

with the bowl of a spoon and paint lemon juice all over pears to prevent discoloration.

Crush Stilton with a fork and work until creamy, then mix with the Shape soft cheese and skimmed milk until smooth. Season to taste.

With a teaspoon, pile cheese mixture into cavities left by the removal of the cores in the pear halves. Sprinkle browned flaked almonds on top and serve on a bed of lettuce.

## Recipe 92
## Grapefruit Fizz

unsweetened grapefruit juice
slimline tonic water

Pour approximately 4 fl oz (100 ml) unsweetened grapefruit juice into a tall glass and add plenty of ice. Add the slimline tonic and continue topping up with the remainder of the tonic.

This drink is an excellent 'filler' before a meal.

## Recipe 93
## St Clements

slimline orange
slimline bitter lemon

Pour half a bottle of each into a tall glass filled with ice. Top up as required.

For an extra special drink use freshly squeezed orange juice with the bitter lemon.

## Recipe 94
### Spritzer

5 fl oz (125 ml) white wine
sparkling mineral water or soda water

Pour the wine into a large size wine glass and add the mineral or soda water. This provides a long and very enjoyable drink that can accompany a meal or just be drunk for pleasure socially.

## Recipe 95
### Caribbean Surprise

5 fl oz (125 ml) unsweetened pineapple juice
1 bottle slimline ginger ale

Mix in a tall glass filled with ice. Top up with ginger ale as desired.
Garnish with a cherry, pineapple, orange slice and pineapple leaves on a cocktail stick.

## Recipe 96
### Ginger Orange

5 fl oz (125 ml) unsweetened orange juice
5 fl oz (125 ml) slimline ginger ale

Mix in a tall glass filled with ice.
Garnish with sliced orange, lemon and mint leaves.

## Recipe 97
## Sludge Gulper

1 can Diet Coke
4 fl oz (100 ml) unsweetened orange juice
ice

Pour orange juice into a tall glass filled with ice. Pour on the Diet Coke.
Serve with a straw.

## Recipe 98
## Hawaii Beach

pineapple juice
squeeze of fresh lemon juice
sparkling mineral water
crushed ice
chopped fresh fruit: banana, orange, pineapple, etc.

Pour the juices into a tall glass, half filled with crushed ice, and serve with chopped fresh fruit.

## Recipe 99
## Buck's Sparkle

orange juice
sparkling mineral water
crushed ice
slices of orange and lemon for garnish

Half fill a tall glass with crushed ice. Pour on the orange juice and sparkling mineral water and garnish with slices of orange and lemon.

# Recipe 100
## Buck's Fizz – The Real Thing!

(*This drink is recommended to celebrate rediscovering your youthful figure*)

1 bottle Champagne, well chilled
freshly squeezed orange juice, well chilled

Fill champagne flutes one-third full with orange juice. Fill to the top with Champagne.

*Cheers!*

# 10
# Exercises, massage creams, treatments . . . do they help?

My Hip and Thigh Diet really does slim hips and thighs very effectively indeed. But can we do any *more* to improve the contours of our trimmed down body?

I believe everyone who is physically able should undertake some form of regular exercise whether it be sport, attending a keep fit class or visiting the gymnasium. No matter how fit or unfit we are we can always find *something* to help us become fitter – even if it's just walking the dog a bit further each day.

Exercise does three things. Firstly, it improves our muscle tone, giving us a much more attractive body shape – and I don't mean we should go to extremes and start body building! No, I mean we look 'healthier' if we have a well toned body rather than an untoned, rather flabby one. It's never too late to start exercising, and even those who are semi-disabled can do some exercises sitting down. The second reason why we should try to exercise regularly is to improve the fitness of our heart. When we exercise we make our heart work harder and it becomes fitter very quickly. Our heart is the most important organ in our body and it is essential that we do all that we can to keep it healthy. We have already discussed how this diet can help reduce the incidence of heart disease, but exercise is just as important. By combining exercise and a low fat diet we are really helping the health of our heart enormously. The third benefit from regular exercise is the fact that it helps to increase our metabolic rate as well as burning up a few more calories. All very important for anyone on a reducing diet.

So exercise is good for us all, both for our looks and our health, but everyone should always check with their doctor first to see that exercise will do you good, not harm. Exercises fall into three basic categories, developing stamina, suppleness or strength or a combination of all three. Jogging, cycling, playing squash, basketball or tennis would be considered stamina activities, whereas yoga, dancing, gymnastics, or judo would develop suppleness. Weight lifting, rowing or digging the garden are strength activities, but of course swimming scores in all three 'S' factors, being a most wonderful sport for almost anyone, even the disabled. I take a Slim 'n' Swim class at the Holiday Inn in my home town of Leicester where ladies of all fitness levels enjoy working out in the safety of water. Those who are recovering from surgery or who suffer from arthritis, rheumatism or whatever find they can do so much more than they could on dry land. The water makes them 'weightless' so the muscles can work freely doing the exercise rather than lifting the body into any activity. I always emphasise that the most important aspect of any exercise must be *enjoyment*. If you don't enjoy something you won't keep it up. Exercise isn't something you should rush into for two mad weeks of activity and then give up because you're fed up! Find an activity that suits you, so that after each session you are looking forward to the next time.

When my first Hip and Thigh Diet proved so successful some of the ladies at my exercise classes said, 'Oh, you won't have time to take our classes soon – you'll be too busy doing more exciting things.' They couldn't be more wrong. I love taking my classes and I love my ladies – a cheerful and friendly crowd if ever there was one! Not only do I enjoy seeing them each week, but actually doing the exercises to pop music in the luxurious surroundings of the Holiday Inn is totally pleasurable. I love it. And that's it – we should *all* aim for enjoyment, not punishment.

So that we can help avoid cellulite, slow, rhythmic or stretching exercises should be undertaken in preference to jogging and jumping-about type exercises. Stretching exercises will encourage muscle tone without jolting the fat cells and therefore encouraging the development of the clusters of sedentary fat cells which form cellulite. In my last book I detailed some exercises that would help tone up hips and thighs and I received many comments from readers saying that they had proved helpful. The problem with exercising from a book is that it is totally impractical and awkward. You're all set in your leotard or tracksuit and have to stop between each exercise to see what you do next! Many readers asked if I could produce an exercise cassette and a video of exercises to complement the Hip and Thigh Diet. When I designed my questionnaire I included a question asking if anyone would be interested in buying such a product if I decided to produce them. The response was an overwhelming 'Yes', so by the time this book is in the bookshops both an exercise cassette with an accompanying poster and a video will be available by mail order.

(Details on how to order can be found on pages 285–88).

People also asked if I held any courses for those seeking additional and personal help and encouragement. I have been running a Postal Slimming Course for many years which proved of great help to those who cannot attend a local slimming group. The principle of the eight-week Postal Course is that in exchange for a fee the slimmer receives a diet, a weight record card and eight diet record sheets which are completed by the slimmer and returned to me. I then forward each completed diet record sheet to one of my very experienced Slimming Consultants who will examine it carefully. The Consultant will then return the diet sheet, with any comments, plus a personal letter of help and encouragement to ensure that the slimmer continues on the right lines. It is very effective and gives the slimmer a 'friend' with whom he or she can share experiences *and* at the same time receive help. After the initial eight-week period, slimmers may continue for a further period, at a reduced rate, if they feel the need. Success is almost inevitable for anyone who enrols on this course because of the personal support they receive from the Consultant.

Details of this service can be found on page 287.

*Massage creams* are the subject of a great deal of debate. Some say they can't work whilst others say they *are* very effective in the treatment of cellulite. I find the whole debate quite interesting, particularly as some say there is no such thing as cellulite! Here is my own personal point of view.

Firstly, anyone who says cellulite doesn't exist obviously doesn't have it and never has had it. I *have* had it – in vast quantities – and still have some. To me there is absolutely no doubt whatsoever that cellulite exists.

Secondly, as my questionnaire team indicated, the Hip and Thigh Diet *did* help to reduce the incidence of this ugly-looking flesh. I also believe that Hip and Thigh massage creams did help to improve the appearance of my own thighs, and would certainly say they are worth a try for anyone who suffers from cellulite. But don't expect miracles – I think they *help* not *cure* the problem. There are a variety of products on the market, from Vichy's Hip and Thigh Cream, Biotherm's Thermo Active 10-Day Contouring Treatment, to Elancyl's Massage Glove and Cream MP24. These treatments aren't cheap, so weigh up the help they might give you against the cost. Perhaps just before your annual holiday you might think about a course of treatment, and put one of these products to the test.

Let us discuss *cellulite* in more detail and see why and how these treatments can help us.

Cellulite is a modified form of fat tissue to be found just below the surface of the skin. It all begins with the stagnation of the blood in capillaries (tiny blood vessels), and this leads to a flow of blood fluids (plasma) through the capillary walls which separate fat-storing cells known as adipose cells. Small groups of these cells become surrounded by collagen fibre bundles in what are known as micronodules. These in turn group together to form macronodules which are responsible for the skin's irregular, wrinkled appearance. It is this uneven appearance that distinguishes cellulite from neighbouring fat on the tummy or waist which is almost always relatively smooth and uniform.

Our bodies use these fat cells and the connective tissue as a kind of storehouse for waste products and because these particular fat cells are metabolically less active than other cells in the body they make an ideal location for whatever toxic waste products the body would like to keep out of the way so that they don't pollute the bloodstream. It is easy to see, therefore, that the problem is a particularly difficult one to solve as the area is partially 'cut off' from our normal circulation.

Consequently these areas are the first to exhibit extra fat and the last to actually reduce.

Men do not suffer with cellulite even when obese. It is a problem only afflicting women and only after puberty, so it is easy to see that the condition is connected with our hormones. Clinical investigations produced evidence that 75% of the women questioned who developed cellulite, did so at a time of hormonal change. In fact 12% developed it at puberty, 17% during pregnancy, 19% when they started taking the birth pill and 27% at the onset of the menopause. The link between the female hormones and predisposition to cellulite becomes even clearer when you consider that oestrogen is also instrumental in controlling fluid retention and this in itself is the crux of the cellulite problem. The female hormonal cycle is finely synchronized with the circulatory system and lympatic drainage in particular, and because faulty circulation is thought to be the root cause of the disorder it is easy to see why massage creams can help. Anything that improves the circulation is therefore one of the answers, but these special creams have the effect of penetrating the skin with plant extracts, going much deeper than ordinary massage creams.

Stress and our inability to cope with it can be an important cellulite trigger because it affects the hypothalamus 'master gland' which controls all other hormonal functions.

Dietary factors also have a very important part to play, as a diet high in junk food encourages the deposit of fat, particularly in the 'waste ground' around our hips, thighs and arms. An excess of foods such as sugar, salt, spices, fat and alcohol can therefore aggravate a cellulite condition by cluttering up the system with additional waste matter that is poorly eliminated. Constipation can also encourage cellulite formation – if the waste matter is not leaving the body through the normal channels the body will store it away from the bloodstream and again the islands of fat cells causing cellulite provide the perfect storehouse.

A diet high in fresh fruit and vegetables is obviously to be recommended as it encourages digestion and elimination. These are also very healthy foods rich in vitamins and minerals. Wholegrain cereals are good for the same reasons, and protein foods (meat, fish, low fat cheese) balance the diet and give all the necessary nutrients. Skimmed milk and low fat spreads should also be preferred to the full fat equivalents in the family diet. Foods high in sugar, salt, fat and spices should be kept to a minimum, and the consumption of alcohol should be restricted too, though there is no need to eliminate it – two drinks a day are acceptable.

Another treatment which can prove helpful in the reduction of cellulite is G5 *Massage*. This is an electrically operated massage machine which gives a penetrating massage action to the affected areas. I find it a pleasant sensation even though it is quite strong. One treatment takes about 20–30 minutes and a course of treatments would be needed to have any positive effect on your shape. Again, I would not say this treatment would have a dramatic effect any more than a massage cream, but it *will* help.

When I decided to write a follow-up book, I realized I needed to investigate more fully such treatments as G5, Slendertone, ordinary body massage, and the treatment creams. In any event, each year I like to spend a few days at a health hydro to experience the pleasure of being on 'the other side' of exercise classes and lectures. Over the years, I have been to several health farms and can honestly say that I have enjoyed them all, but for different reasons. In my view it certainly doesn't follow that the more you pay the better it is, but they *all* have their individual merits.

Health hydros operate in a variety of ways. Some include all the treatments in the weekly tariff, but others offer you a minimum of treatments included in the price, with any additional ones charged extra. I recently spent a week at Inglewood Health Hydro in Kintbury, Berkshire, where you are given a choice of a variety of treatments and activities, and your daily timetable is designed around your personal requirements. These treatments are included in your weekly rate. Because of my particular interest in surface treatments for hips and thighs I opted for a daily special bath (usually seaweed), body massage, G5 treatment and Slendertone passive exercise therapy. These were in addition to exercise, yoga, relaxation and pool sessions.

In all the health farms or hydros I have ever attended you would not have had the opportunity to be given *all* of these treatments *every day*. In fact, if someone said to me, 'What is the absolute maximum I could do in a week to help my hips and thighs?' I would say, follow a low fat diet, and each day exercise, have a heat treatment (e.g. bath, sauna, steam) followed by a massage, G5 treatment and Slendertone, and a brisk walk.

*Passive exercise machines*: A passive exercise machine exercises muscles while you lie on a couch or bed. A portable machine running on batteries is available, or a larger electrically powered 'salon' model. Both come supplied with full instructions for correct usage.

The portable machine consists of an operating unit plus eight plastic-covered wires which in turn are connected to round rubber pads. The pads are placed at strategic points on your body (depending on which part you wish to tone), and are held in place with wide elasticated bands. The machine works on the body by activating the muscles you wish to tone without physical movement. Your legs may *feel* like they have walked 30 miles at the end of your 40-minute session, but you won't have sore feet or feel at all tired!

This all sounds too good to be true, but there are certain disadvantages. The machines are not cheap, and are very time-consuming. They are extremely inconvenient if someone calls unexpectedly at your door!

No passive exercise machine will eliminate fat. You can only do that by reducing your energy input by calorie cutting and increasing your energy output by taking real exercise. However they can help your muscle shape, and they will certainly make your long-lost muscles come back to life, so if for any reason you can't take normal exercise, a machine could be invaluable to you. For some people they work very well, but not everyone can tolerate the strange sensation given out by some of these machines.

So, to sum up, the answer must be 'yes' to all of these activities; the right sort of exercise will definitely tone you up; massage creams and other treatments will encourage improved circulation and, to a limited degree, *will* help. Several slimmers wrote to me saying that they had undertaken a course of G5 massage treatment after losing weight and inches on the diet, and they felt it definitely helped to improve their shape and tone them up.

# 11
# The Maintenance Programme

Losing weight is ironically always the easiest part of weight control partly because of the novelty value and partly because the instructions that we have to follow are quite clear. The problems arise once we *stop* dieting. Suddenly we feel free from the restrictions that have been placed upon us and it is all too easy to think, 'Great. I can now eat chocolate, chips and cakes!' In this respect the Hip and Thigh Diet is more helpful, because you cannot return to eating lots of the foods that made you fat in the first place – that is if you want to keep your new slimmer and trimmer figure. But you *can* relax a little and you *can* eat a wider variety of foods, including eggs, low fat Cheddar cheese and fatless cakes.

On most diets the metabolic rate falls because the body adjusts to a reduced calorie intake and when people return to 'normal' eating the weight piles back on even though they are not over-eating. It all seems so unfair doesn't it? Fortunately, because the Hip and Thigh Diet offers so much food – more calories than most diets would allow – the metabolic rate hardly falls at all. This is particularly evident with those who undertake regular exercise.

We lose weight when we consume fewer calories than our body needs, and we therefore make up the deficit from our stores of fat. After reaching our desired weight, we need to feed our body sufficient calories to maintain that new weight, but not ruin all our good work by eating too much and storing the remainder as fat again. It is a tricky situation, but so long as you keep a careful eye on the tape measure and the scales, you will soon become more confident in your ability to keep your weight constant. If you do over-indulge and you do gain weight, by returning to the diet for a few days you should be able to undo the damage quite quickly. But, if you wish to retain your slimmer hips and thighs, you must realize that a low fat diet in the long term is essential. I don't think you need to worry too much with this point, however, as so many of my correspondents stated that their taste buds had been completely re-educated after following the diet – as were my own – and it was no effort at all to maintain their new figures. Many in fact completed questionnaires after they had been on the Maintenance Programme and they commented that with previous diets they had always regained the lost weight very quickly, but this time it was quite a different story. I could sense they were confident that they would never return to their bad, high fat, eating habits ever again.

With all this in mind it is clear that this chapter is a very important one. It is vital to learn which foods may be eaten freely and which should be avoided so that we can have slim hips and thighs for ever!

You may prefer to release yourself from the restrictions of an actual diet. If so, please read carefully the following four pages. They explain your nutritional requirements and which foods may be reintroduced into your daily diet, together with those which should still be avoided.

There is no need to tot up your daily intake of grams of fat. If you follow the basic principles already learned whilst on the diet, you really have nothing to fear. It is only when you start breaking the rules about forbidden foods on a regular basis that you will undo the good results that you have achieved. The very fact that we have avoided the need to count any form of units or calories throughout the diet has weaned us away from this negative habit. It would be a shame to start now with the counting of grams of fat. So relax and just remember what you've learned so far.

The following lists of foods and recommendations should form the pattern of foods consumed for a healthy diet. A daily diet made up of reasonable quantities from each category will ensure a balanced consumption of essential nutrients to maintain health and energy, without including unnecessary foods which add useless calories and lead to unwanted fat. A diet which follows these recommendations will encourage a healthy digestion, and constipation problems will become a thing of the past.

## Protein and minerals

A minimum of 6 oz (175 g) of meat, fish, eggs or cheese should be consumed daily.

½ pint (250 ml) skimmed or semi-skimmed milk should be consumed daily – maximum 1 pint (500 ml) per day.

| | | |
|---|---|---|
| Fish | Any type | Steamed, grilled or microwaved without fat |
| Meat | Any type, lean cuts only | Grilled, roast or microwaved, without fat, and with all fat trimmed off before cooking, or trimmed afterwards |
| Poultry | Any type | Grilled, roast or microwaved, without fat. Do not eat any skin or fat |
| Offal | Any type | Steamed, baked or microwaved, without fat |
| Eggs | | Cook in any way without the use of fat. Consume no more than 4 per week |
| Cheese | Preferably low fat e.g. Shape, Tendale, Edam | Restrict to 4 oz (100 g) per week if possible |
| Cheese | Cottage | Unlimited quantities may be consumed |
| Yogurt | Any type | Unlimited |

## Vitamins

Approx. 12 oz (350 g) of fruit or vegetables should be consumed daily.

| | | |
|---|---|---|
| Vegetables | Any type | Unlimited, but always without butter |
| Fruit | Any type | Unlimited. Serve on its own, or with Shape Single or top of the milk or ice cream |

## Carbohydrates
A minimum of 4 oz (100 g) to be consumed daily.

| | | |
|---|---|---|
| Bread | Wholemeal or Crispbreads | Unlimited if eaten without fat; otherwise limit consumption to 3 slices of bread a day or 8 crispbreads |
| Cereal | Breakfast | 1–2 oz (25–50 g) per day |
| Rice | Brown | 2 oz (50 g) per day |
| Pasta | Fat free | Average portions 2–3 oz (50–75 g) |
| Potatoes | Boiled or baked | Unlimited if eaten without fat |

## Fats
Consume as little as possible.

| | | |
|---|---|---|
| Low fat spread | Gold Outline Gold Lowest | Maximum of ½ oz (12 g) per day only. No butter or margarine |
| Cream | Single | 1–2 oz (25–50 g) very occasionally |

## In addition, the following foods may be eaten in moderation
Milk puddings made with skimmed milk

Reduced-oil salad dressings, e.g. Waistline or Heinz Weight Watchers

Cakes made without fat (see Recipe 76, page 187, Apple Gâteau and Recipe 89, page 193, Bran Cake)

Ice cream

Pancakes made with skimmed milk

Yorkshire pudding made with skimmed milk in non-stick baking tin

Trifle made with only fatless sponge and custard made with skimmed milk, no cream
Cauliflower cheese made with low fat cheese and skimmed milk
Sausages, if grilled well
Nuts – only very few and avoid Brazils, Barcelona nuts or almonds
Horlicks, Ovaltine or Drinking Chocolate
Sauces if possible made with skimmed milk, but *no* butter
Soups excepting cream soups
Soya, low fat type

**Avoid the following foods**
Butter, margarine, Flora, or similar products
Oil, lard, dripping, etc.
Soya, full fat type
Fried bread
Chapatis made with fat
Biscuits, all sweet varieties
Cakes, all except fat-free recipes
Milk, dried, whole
Cream, double, whipping, sterilized, canned
Cheese, all types except Edam, cottage, Tendale or Shape low fat Cheddar
Cheese spread
Quiches, Scotch eggs, cheese soufflé, Welsh Rarebit, etc.
Fat from meat, streaky bacon
Skin from chicken, turkey, duck, goose, etc.
Salami, pâté, pork pie, meat pies, etc.
Sprats or whitebait, fried
Fish in oil
Anything fried, including mushrooms or onions
Dessicated coconut

Brazil nuts, almonds, Barcelona nuts
Chocolate, toffees, fudge, caramel, butterscotch
Mayonnaise
Marzipan
French dressing made with oil
Pastries
Pork scratchings
Avocados

Many of my slimmers so enjoyed the menus offered on the Hip and Thigh Diet that it became obvious that a Maintenance Programme including these meals should be designed. Also, some people prefer to read in black and white exactly what options are open to them. For those slimmers I have adjusted the whole range of Diet Menu suggestions listed earlier in the book. Weight maintenance has never been so easy to achieve.

To some degree you can adjust these menus to suit your own individual needs and circumstances, but bear in mind that at the end of the day calories do count so don't substitute a bowl of cornflakes for half a grapefruit! It may take a week or two for your body to adjust to the increased allowance of food so keep a careful eye on the scales and tape measure. Gradually work your way into the Maintenance Menu suggestions. You will then realize how much you *can* eat and not gain weight. The only real danger area is when you are out for a meal and have no option but to eat food which is high in fat. Even when you have achieved your desired weight you should always remember to cut down after such a meal, to counteract the potential damage that could be done.

## Maintenance Diet instructions

You may select from the following menus three meals per day – a breakfast, lunch and a three-course dinner.

You may consume up to 1 pint (500 ml) skimmed or semi-skimmed milk.

Fresh fruit may be eaten freely as desired.

## Maintenance Programme

### Cereal breakfasts

Served with skimmed milk and 2 teaspoons brown sugar if desired.

1. 1 oz (25 g) porridge oats, made with water, served with 2 teaspoons of honey, plus one piece of fruit.
2. Home-made muesli (see Recipe 1, page 137) plus ½ slice toast and 1 teaspoon orange marmalade.
3. 1 oz (25 g) bran flakes or bran flakes with sultanas, plus ½ slice toast and 1 teaspoon orange marmalade.
4. 1 oz (25 g) cornflakes, puffed rice, sugar flakes or rye and raisin cereal, plus a diet yogurt.
5. 2 Weetabix, plus a piece of fruit.
6. 1 oz (25 g) whole wheat cereal, plus a piece of fruit.

### Fruit breakfasts

N.B. 'Diet yogurt' means low fat, low calorie yogurt.

1. 1 banana plus 5 oz (150 g) non-diet yogurt or two diet yogurts – any flavour.
2. 4 oz (100 g) tinned peaches in natural juice plus 5 oz (150 g) diet yogurt – any flavour, plus ½ slice of toast and 1 teaspoon marmalade.
3. 5 prunes in natural juice plus 5 oz (150 g) natural yogurt and ½ slice of toast with 1 teaspoon marmalade.
4. 5 prunes in natural juice plus 1 slice of toast with 1 teaspoon marmalade.
5. 4 dried apricots, soaked and 4 prunes (see Recipe 2, page 137) plus 5 oz (150 g) diet yogurt – any flavour.
6. As much fresh fruit as you can eat at one sitting.
7. 8 oz (225 g) stewed fruit, (cooked without sugar) plus a diet yogurt – any flavour.
8. 6 oz (175 g) fruit compote (e.g. oranges, grapefruit, peaches, pineapple, pears – all in natural juice) plus a yogurt.
9. 10 oz (275 g) tinned grapefruit in natural juice plus ½ slice of toast and 1 teaspoon of marmalade.
10. 1 whole fresh grapefruit plus 1 slice of toast and marmalade.

## Cooked and continental breakfasts

1. 1 scrambled egg and a small can of tomatoes served on 1½ slices (1½ oz) [37 g] toast.
2. 8 oz (225 g) tinned tomatoes served on 2 slices (2 oz) [50 g] toast.
3. 2 oz (50 g) very lean bacon (all fat removed)

served with unlimited tinned tomatoes, plus a slice of toast.
4. ½ grapefruit plus 1 slice (1 oz) [25 g] toast with a boiled egg.
5. 6 oz (175 g) smoked haddock, steamed in skimmed milk, plus a poached egg.
6. 2 oz (50 g) lean ham, 2 tomatoes plus 1 fresh wholemeal bread roll and a low fat spread or 2 teaspoons of jam.
7. 2 oz (50 g) cured chicken or turkey breast, 2 tomatoes, plus 1 fresh wholemeal roll and 2 teaspoons of jam or marmalade.
8. 2 oz (50 g) smoked turkey breast plus 1 fresh wholemeal roll and a little low fat spread.
9. 1 oz (25 g) very lean bacon (all fat removed) served with 4 oz (100 g) mushrooms cooked in vegetable stock, 3 oz (75 g) baked beans, 8 oz (225 g) tinned tomatoes or 4 fresh tomatoes grilled and a dry-fried or poached egg.
10. 1 oz (25 g) very lean bacon (all fat removed), 4 oz (100 g) mushrooms cooked in stock, 8 oz (200 g) tinned tomatoes or 4 fresh tomatoes grilled plus a slice (1 oz) [25 g] of toast.

## Fruit lunches

1. Pineapple boat (see Recipe 3, page 138) plus a diet yogurt or scoop of ice cream.
2. Prawn and Grapefruit Cocktail (see Recipe 4, page 138) plus fruit or a diet yogurt.
3. 4–5 pieces of any fruit (e.g. 1 orange, 1 pear, 1 apple, 1 plum) plus a yogurt.
4. 8 oz (225 g) fresh fruit salad topped with a little scoop of ice cream or Shape Single.

5. 3 pieces of any fresh fruit plus 2 diet yogurts.

## Packed lunches

1. 2 slices of bread, spread with reduced-oil salad dressing, piled with lettuce, salad and prawns, plus a diet yogurt or piece of fresh fruit.
2. Contents of a small can of baked beans, plus a chopped salad of lettuce, tomatoes, onions, celery, cucumber, etc., and a hard boiled egg.
3. 2 slices of bread filled with 2 oz (50 g) ham, lettuce, cucumber, tomato, pickle and mustard.
4. 5 Ryvitas spread with 2 oz (50 g) pickle and 5 slices of turkey roll or chicken roll, or 3 oz (75 g) ordinary chicken or turkey breast, plus 2 tomatoes sliced and 1 piece of fruit.
5. Chicken leg (no skin), chopped salad, Carrot Salad (see Recipe 12, page 142), soy sauce or Worcestershire sauce and dressed with natural yogurt, plus a piece of fresh fruit or a cup-a-soup.
6. 5 Ryvitas spread with low fat cottage cheese, topped with prawns, plus a piece of fruit.
7. 5 Ryvitas spread thinly with Shape low fat soft cheese and topped with salad and prawns or chopped chicken.
8. 4 oz (100 g) red kidney beans, 4 oz (100 g) sweetcorn, plus chopped cucumber, tomatoes, onions tossed in mint sauce and natural yogurt, plus a cup-a-soup or 1 piece of fresh fruit.
9. 4 low fat, low calorie yogurts – any flavour, plus 2 pieces of fresh fruit.

10. Salad of lettuce, tomato, cucumber, onion, grated carrot, etc., plus prawns, shrimps, cockles, lobster, crab (6 oz) [175 g] total seafood). Seafood Dressing (see Recipe 5, page 139), plus a piece of fresh fruit or 1 cup-a-soup.
11. 4 Ryvitas spread with any flavour low fat cottage cheese, topped with tomatoes plus unlimited salad vegetables. 1 slimmers' cup-a-soup.
12. 3 Ryvitas with low fat cottage cheese or soft cheese, topped with salad vegetables, plus 1 diet yogurt.
13. 1 slimmer's cup-a-soup. 3 pieces of fresh fruit, plus 1 diet yogurt.
14. 1 slimmer's cup-a-soup. 1 slice of bread spread with a dessertspoon of reduced oil dressing and topped with salad and 2 oz (50 g) grated low fat Cheddar – e.g. Shape or Tendale.
15. Triple decker sandwich – with 3 slices of bread filled with 1 oz (25 g) turkey or chicken roll and 2 oz (50 g) cottage cheese, lettuce, tomatoes, cucumber, sliced Spanish onion. Spread bread with oil-free sweet pickle of your choice (e.g. Branston or mustard, ketchup or reduced-oil salad dressing). Make one sandwich with chicken or turkey and salad, spread other slice of bread with cottage cheese and salad and place other sandwich on top.
16. 4 Ryvitas spread with 2 oz (50 g) pilchards in tomato sauce, topped with sliced tomato, plus a piece of fresh fruit.
17. 3 slices wholemeal bread spread with Seafood Dressing (see Recipe 5, page 139) made into

sandwiches with 2 oz (50 g) tinned salmon and cucumber, plus a piece of fresh fruit.

## Cold lunches

1. 1 cup-a-soup, Curried Chicken and Yogurt Salad (see Recipe 6, page 139).
2. Seafood Salad (see Recipe 7, page 139) plus fresh fruit salad or yogurt.
3. Cheese, Prawn and Asparagus Salad (see Recipe 8, page 140) plus 1 piece of fresh fruit or yogurt.
4. Chicken joint (with skin removed) or prawns, served with a chopped salad of lettuce, cucumber, radish, spring onions, peppers, tomatoes, with reduced oil dressing, or yogurt dressing, plus 1 piece of fresh fruit.
5. Crab and asparagus open sandwiches: 2 slices wholemeal bread spread with Seafood Dressing (see Recipe 5, page 139). Spread fresh or tinned crab meat, or seafood sticks, on to the bread and decorate with asparagus spears. Plus fresh fruit salad.
6. Orange and Carrot Salad (see Recipe 10, page 141), plus a yogurt.
7. Red Kidney Bean Salad (see Recipe 11, page 141), plus a yogurt.
8. 4 slices wholemeal bread made into jumbo sandwiches. Spread bread with reduced oil salad dressing and fill with lots of salad vegetables, e.g. lettuce, cucumber, onion, cress, tomatoes, beetroot, green and red peppers.
9. 4 oz (100 g) cottage cheese (any flavour)

served with large assorted salad. 1 yogurt and 1 piece of fresh fruit.

10. Large salad served with prawns and 1 hard boiled egg and dressed with Seafood Dressing (see Recipe 5, page 139).

11. Rice salad: a bowl of chopped peppers, tomatoes, onion, peas, sweetcorn, ½ oz (12 g) peanuts and cucumber mixed with cooked (boiled) brown rice. Served with soy sauce.

12. 8 oz (225 g) carton low fat cottage cheese, any flavour, with two tinned pear halves, chopped apple and celery, served on a bed of lettuce and garnished with tomato and cucumber; plus a yogurt.

13. 3 oz (75 g) pilchards in tomato sauce, served with a large salad, and lemon vinaigrette dressing or reduced-oil salad dressing, plus fresh fruit salad.

14. 3 oz (75 g) salmon served with a large salad and mint yogurt dressing or reduced-oil salad dressing and a fresh fruit salad or piece of fresh fruit.

15. Mixed salad served with 4 oz (100 g) diet coleslaw, e.g. Shape – any flavour, plus 4 oz (100 g) pot of potato salad, plus 2 oz (50 g) prawns or 2 oz (50 g) chicken, plus 1 piece of fresh fruit.

16. 5 Ryvitas spread with low calorie coleslaw (e.g. Shape) any flavour, and topped with salad, plus 1 piece of fresh fruit or a diet yogurt.

## Hot lunches

1. Pea and Ham Soup (see Recipe 14, page 142), plus a slice of wholemeal toast.
2. Jacket potato topped with 8 oz (225 g) tin baked beans and ½ oz (12 g) grated low fat cheese or a piece of fresh fruit.
3. 2 slices (2 oz [50 g]) wholemeal toast with 15 oz (425 g) tin baked beans, plus a piece of fresh fruit.
4. Jacket potato served with low fat cottage cheese and salad (cottage cheese may be flavoured with chives, onion, pineapple, etc., but it must be 'low fat'), plus a piece of fresh fruit.
5. 1 cup-a-soup, plus 2 baked, stuffed apples filled with 1 oz (25 g) dried fruit, a few breadcrumbs and sweetened with honey or artificial sweetener, served with plain low fat yogurt.
6. Clear or vegetable soup, served with one slice of toast followed by 2 pieces fresh fruit and a yogurt.
7. Jacket potato with 2 oz (50 g) roast beef, pork or ham (with all fat removed) or 4 oz (100 g) chicken (no skin), served with Branston pickle and salad and a little reduced oil dressing.
8. 2 slices wholemeal toast with small tin baked beans and small tin tomatoes, plus a piece of fresh fruit.
9. Jacket potato served with sweetcorn and chopped salad and reduced oil dressing.
10. Jacket potato served with grated carrot, chopped onion, tomatoes, sweetcorn and

peppers, topped with low fat coleslaw, plus 1 yogurt.
11. Jacket potato filled with 4 oz (100 g) cottage cheese mixed with 4 teaspoons tomato purée and black pepper, plus a yogurt or a piece of fresh fruit.
12. Jacket potato with 4 oz (100 g) pot of Shape prawn coleslaw, plus 1 piece of fresh fruit.
13. Jacket potato with 4 oz (100 g) Shape coleslaw and a diet yogurt.
14. Jacket potato with 4 oz (100 g) Shape 1000 Island coleslaw, plus a piece of fresh fruit.
15. Jacket potato with 4 oz (100 g) Shape Garlic and Herb coleslaw, plus a piece of fresh fruit.
16. Jacket potato with kidney in Barbecue Sauce (see Recipe 15, page 143), plus a diet yogurt.
17. Jacket Potato with Chicken and Peppers (see Recipe 16, page 143), plus a piece of fresh fruit.
18. 1 cup-a-soup and 1 Jacket Potato with Prawns and Sweetcorn (see Recipe 18, page 144).

## Dinner: starters

1. Crudités (see Recipe 19, page 145), plus an extra glass of wine if desired or small bread roll.
2. Chicken and Mushrooom Soup – (see Recipe 20, page 145), plus ½ slice wholemeal toast.
3. Orange and Grapefruit Cocktail (see Recipe 21, page 146), plus small bread roll.
4. Melon and Prawn Salad (see Recipe 22, page 146), plus small bread roll.
5. Pair of Pears (see Recipe 23, page 147), plus extra glass of wine if desired.

6. French Tomatoes (see Recipe 24, page 147), plus ½ slice wholemeal bread spread with low fat spread.
7. Grapefruit segments in natural juice, plus wholemeal roll.
8. Melon balls in slimline ginger ale, plus an extra glass of wine if desired.
9. Clear soup with a small bread roll.
10. Garlic Mushrooms (see Recipe 25, page 148), plus a small bread roll.
11. Melon Salad (see Recipe 26, page 149), plus garlic bread.
12. Ratatouille (see Recipe 27, page 150), plus garlic bread.
13. Wedge of melon, plus extra glass of wine.
14. Half a grapefruit, plus extra glass of wine.
15. Stilton Pears (see Recipe 91, page 194).

N.B. *The suggested extra glass of wine may be exchanged for a small wholemeal roll to suit individual tastes.*

## Dinner: main courses

For those following the Maintenance Programme, select from the following suggested menus relaxing to some degree as far as quantities are concerned.

1. Stir-fried Chicken and Vegetables (see Recipe 29, page 151).
2. Haddock Florentine (see Recipe 30, page 151) with potatoes.
3. Chicken Veronique (see Recipe 31, page 152) with potatoes and onions.
4. Tandoori Chicken (see Recipe 33, page 154).
5. Shepherds' Pie (see Recipe 34, page 155).
6. Fish Curry with rice (see Recipe 35, page 156).

7. Steak Surprise (see Recipe 36, page 157).
8. Steamed, grilled or microwaved white fish (cod, plaice, whiting, haddock, lemon sole, halibut) served with unlimited boiled vegetables.
9. Chicken joint baked with skin removed, in Barbecue Sauce (see Recipe 37, page 157) and served with jacket potato or boiled brown rice and vegetables of your choice.
10. Scous (see Recipe 38, page 158).
11. Spaghetti Bolognese (see Recipe 39, page 159).
12. Barbecued Chicken or Turkey Kebabs (see Recipe 40, page 160) served with boiled brown rice.
13. Roast leg of pork with all fat removed, served with apple sauce and unlimited vegetables.
14. Steamed or grilled or microwaved trout, stuffed with prawns and served with a large salad or assorted vegetables.
15. Calves', ox, pigs' or lamb's liver, braised with onions, and served with unlimited vegetables.
16. Turkey (no skin) served with cranberry sauce, dry roast potatoes, and unlimited vegetables.
17. Roast lamb with all fat removed, served with Dry-roast Parsnips (see Recipe 82, page 190) and unlimited vegetables.
18. Chicken (no skin) steamed, grilled, baked or microwaved, and served with unlimited vegetables.
19; Chicken or Prawn Chop Suey (see Recipe 41, page 161) served with boiled brown rice.
20. Chicken Curry (see Recipe 43, page 162), served with boiled brown rice.

21. Grilled or baked gammon steak or gammon rashers, with all fat removed, served with pineapple and unlimited vegetables.
22. Fish Pie (see Recipe 44, page 163) served with unlimited vegetables.
23. Bacon grilled, with all fat removed, served with grilled tomatoes, baked beans and jacket or boiled potatoes.
24. Roast duck (all skin removed) served with unlimited vegetables.
25. Chinese Chicken (see Recipe 45, page 164).
26. Fish Risotto (see Recipe 46, page 165).
27. Steak – rump or sirloin, grilled, and served with a jacket potato or very few chips, plus salad or vegetables.

## Dinner: vegetarian main courses

1 oz (25 g) low fat cheese may be included with any of the following recipes, as desired. Alternatively, ½ oz (12 g) nuts or one egg may be added in whatever form you wish.

1. Stuffed Marrow (see Recipe 47, page 166) served with unlimited vegetables.
2. Vegetable Bake (see Recipe 48, page 166).
3. Vegetarian Shepherds' Pie (see Recipe 50, page 168) served with unlimited vegetables.
4. Vegetable Curry (see Recipe 51, page 169) served on a bed of boiled brown rice.
5. Vegetarian Chilli con Carne (see Recipe 52, page 169) served on a bed of boiled brown rice.
6. Vegetable Chilli (see Recipe 53, page 170) served on a bed of boiled brown rice.

7. Vegetarian Spaghetti Bolognese (see Recipe 54, page 171).
8. Mushroom Stroganoff (see Recipe 55, page 172) served with unlimited vegetables.
9. Bean Salad (see Recipe 56, page 172) served with cold boiled brown rice and soy sauce.
10. Hummus with Crudités (see Recipe 57, page 173).
11. Spiced Bean Casserole (see Recipe 58, page 174) served with unlimited vegetables.
12. Vegetable Kebabs (see Recipe 59, page 175) served on a bed of rice and sweetcorn.
13. Vegetable Casserole (see Recipe 60, page 176) served with boiled brown rice or Lyonnaise Potatoes (see Recipe 32, page 154).
14. Three Bean Salad (see Recipe 61, page 177) served with salad and cold boiled brown rice.
15. Stuffed Peppers (see Recipe 62, page 177) served with salad.
16. Black Eye Bean Casserole (see Recipe 63, page 178).
17. Chick Pea and Fennel Casserole (see Recipe 64, page 179).
18. Vegetable Chop Suey (see Recipe 42, page 162) served with boiled brown rice.
19. Vegetarian Goulash (see Recipe 49, page 167).

**Dinner: desserts**

1. Meringue basket filled with raspberries and topped with raspberry yogurt or 1 scoop ice cream.
2. Fruit Sundae (see Recipe 65, page 179), plus a tablespoon Shape Single.

3. Stuffed apple served with plain yogurt or ice cream.
4. 4 oz (100 g) fresh fruit salad mixed with 4 oz (100 g) natural yogurt or 2 oz (50 g) Shape Single or scoop ice cream.
5. Stewed fruit (cooked without sugar) served with 3 oz (75g) Low Fat Custard (see Recipe 66, page 180) or ice cream.
6. Apple and Blackcurrant Whip (see Recipe 67, page 180), plus Shape Single.
7. Pineapple and Orange Sorbet (see Recipe 68, page 181), plus Shape Single.
8. Raspberry Mousse (see Recipe 69, page 181), plus Shape Single or ice cream.
9. Sliced banana topped with fresh raspberries, plus 1 tablespoon Shape Double or 1 scoop ice cream.
10. Fresh strawberries or raspberries served with Shape Double (2 tablespoons).
11. Pears in Red Wine (see Recipe 70, page 182) served with Shape Single.
12. Pineapple in Kirsch (see Recipe 71, page 183) served with ice cream.
13. Oranges in Cointreau (see Recipe 72, page 183) served with Shape Single.
14. Sliced banana topped with fresh raspberries or strawberries, plus a diet yogurt.
15. Fresh peaches sliced and served with fresh raspberries and a scoop of ice cream.
16. Two pieces of fruit of your choice, plus a diet yogurt.
17. Pineapple Boat (see Recipe 3, page 138) served with 1 scoop pineapple ice cream.
18. Diet Rice Pudding (see Recipe 73, page 184),

plus 1 tablespoon of jam or 3 oz (75 g) tinned fruit in natural juice.
19. Fruit Sorbet (see Recipe 74, page 185), plus 1 scoop any flavour ice cream.
20. Pears in Meringue (see Recipe 75, page 186) served with a little Shape Single.
21. 8 oz (200 g) fresh fruit salad, served with 1 scoop ice cream or Shape Single.
22. Diet yogurt, including French style set yogurt, served on a scoop of ice cream.
23. Stewed rhubarb sweetened with artificial sweetener, served with rhubarb diet yogurt, and ice cream.
24. Low fat fromage frais – e.g. Shape – any flavour.
25. Piece Apple Gâteau with Shape Single (see Recipe 76, page 187).
26. 1 slice of Bran Cake (see Recipe 89, page 193).

## Drinks

Tea and coffee may be drunk freely if drunk black, or may be drunk white using skimmed or semi-skimmed milk. Use artificial sweetener whenever possible, though on the maintenance programme a little sugar may be taken.

Unless otherwise stated in the menus, your alcohol allowance of two drinks per day remains unchanged but drinks may be 'saved up' as required. 1 drink means a single measure of any spirits, a glass of wine, or small glass of sherry or half a pint of beer or lager. Slimline mixers and Diet drinks should be used whenever possible and these may be drunk freely.

You may drink as much water as you like.

Grape, apple, unsweetened orange, grapefruit, pineapple, exotic fruit juices may be drunk in moderation. The recipes for low calorie drinks detailed on pages 195–198 are still ideal for the maintenance programme.

## Sauces, gravy, spreads and dressings

Sauces made without fat, and with low fat skimmed milk from the daily allowance, may be eaten. Thicker gravy made with gravy powder, but not granules, may also be served with main courses. Marmite or Bovril may be used freely to add flavour to cooking and on bread. For salads select any of the fat free dressings (see recipes). You can have the seafood dressing and reduced-oil salad dressing as desired.

# 12
# Living life to the full

Overweight can cause us to have such a low opinion of ourselves that we can easily lose out on our true potential. We learned in an earlier chapter how some of my slimmers had found confidence to embark on a new life after acquiring a new figure – one with which they felt happy – and surely this must be true of everyone.

I believe we all have a talent. For some it may be flower arranging or decorating, others may find they are a dab hand at organizing, some may have a flair in business or writing poetry, sewing or knitting, teaching, communicating or supporting – a million and one options to choose from! Your talent may be obvious to you already but, as yet, you haven't had the courage to develop it properly – or perhaps you fancy having a go at something but so far just haven't had the nerve.

With a new, happy and healthy attitude to life, now is the time to give it a try. You may decide to book into your local night school, start taking driving lessons, go back to work or start a business. Until you try you'll have no idea of your natural ability and you *could* be brilliantly successful. If you *don't* try you won't ever know and as someone very wisely put it, 'You get paid for doing, not dreaming.' So don't just sit about thinking about it – do it! Get rid of excuses and eliminate from your vocabulary the words 'I can't'. And as the old saying goes, 'If at first you don't succeed, try and try again.' If you try hard enough you are almost bound to succeed.

If we aren't happy with ourselves we will *never* realize our true potential and then we *will* feel a failure, so when those people who *don't* have a weight problem criticize those of us who do and who try to lose weight, I don't think they realize how important it is psychologically for us to feel happy about ourselves. A slim body is very important indeed to some people – we must accept that. Paradoxically it is those of us who suffer with a weight problem who desperately *need* to be slim. Those who are naturally slim just don't understand how we feel.

When we have more confidence we are able to sort out our lives – those problems that previously we felt unable to solve. Many who are basically unhappy put up with that unhappiness for years just because they lack self-confidence. In my talks I describe life as a garden. Our garden of life can be full of flowers or full of weeds and if we are to achieve real happiness we should remove the 'weeds' one by one and replace them with flowers. Perhaps the problem might be a selfish next door neighbour; a boss who you feel hates you, so that you dread going to work; a relative who really gets you down or a job that you loathe. Whatever it is, it won't get better unless you do something about it.

When we have more confidence we can stand up to people so much better, and make our own views known. Most of the time the person who is actually getting on our nerves has absolutely no idea that there *is* a problem at all. So, the sooner we can discuss it the better! We shouldn't use bulldozer tactics to clear away the weeds, because if we do we will hurt people and that's the *last* thing we want to do. But by thoughtfully putting our point across – as soon as possible – you'd be amazed how understanding and co-operative people can be.

Aggression is often displayed as a compensation for a lack of confidence. As soon as you become polite and charming – though it must of course be sincere – the world becomes a most wonderful place in which to live. I try to build up the confidence of anyone I can. When slimmers have been coming to my classes for a few weeks, I begin to see a flower blossoming. Sometimes they start exercising in a tracksuit but later on, when they have lost some weight, they have the confidence to wear a leotard. I try to make a point of saying how much slimmer they look – I can *see* when they've lost weight. When I tell them, they are positively thrilled and they are like a flower growing. It is beautiful to see.

We all love to receive compliments, but oh, the joy of *giving* them. If you have the confidence to compliment people, you will find everyone is so friendly. So I believe it is a very good thing to get into the habit of complimenting people. And if you are fortunate enough to be on the receiving end, do accept the compliment as if it were a gift – graciously and with gratitude. Don't shrug it off. When you have lost all those inches on the Hip and Thigh Diet and someone says, 'You look fantastic,' please say 'Thank you!' and enjoy it!

# 13
# A guide to fat in food – the complete tables

The following tables list the average fat content of everyday foods which are available in shops or served in restaurants, and illustrate, at a glance, the fat content for easy reading and learning.

The tables do not include the fat content of the recipes included in this book. These recipes have been carefully designed to reduce as much fat as possible and are therefore considerably lower in fat content in comparison with 'standard recipes'.

By comparing suggested meals listed in Chapter 8, alternative meals may be designed to suit your own individual tastes, bearing in mind the fat content of the various foods. Some foods, of course, are low in fat but high in calories, so a certain amount of commonsense is needed to ensure that you do not overeat and gain weight. For instance alcohol and boiled sweets contain no fat, but they contain loads of calories, so their consumption should be moderated!

As a rule of thumb for those following the Maintenance Programme, try to select foods from the tables which have a fat content of not more than 4 grams per ounce.

The food tables have been drawn up to indicate the fat content of 25 grams of each item listed and for the sake of convenience I have taken 25 grams to equal one ounce instead of the actual equivalent of 28.349 grams to the ounce. The reason for this is that most products are labelled with the composition per 100 grams and my tables are therefore based on a quarter of this value.

By reading these tables you will learn quickly which foods are high and which are low in fat and after a while you will be able to steer an easy course to healthy eating and a long and active life.

# FAT TABLES

# Grams per 25g/1oz (approx)

| | 1 | 2 | 3 | 4 | 5 | 6 | 7 | 8 | 9 | 10 | 11 | 12 | 13 | 14 | 15 | 16 | 17 | 18 | 19 | 20 | 21 | 22 | 23 | 24 | 25 |
|---|---|---|---|---|---|---|---|---|---|---|---|---|---|---|---|---|---|---|---|---|---|---|---|---|---|
| **ALCOHOL** | | | | | | | | | | | | | | | | | | | | | | | | | |
| **Beers:** | | | | | | | | | | | | | | | | | | | | | | | | | |
| Brown Ale | • | | | | | | | | | | | | | | | | | | | | | | | | |
| Canned Beer | • | | | | | | | | | | | | | | | | | | | | | | | | |
| Draught | • | | | | | | | | | | | | | | | | | | | | | | | | |
| Keg | • | | | | | | | | | | | | | | | | | | | | | | | | |
| Lager | • | | | | | | | | | | | | | | | | | | | | | | | | |
| Pale Ale | • | | | | | | | | | | | | | | | | | | | | | | | | |
| Stout | • | | | | | | | | | | | | | | | | | | | | | | | | |
| Stout, Extra | • | | | | | | | | | | | | | | | | | | | | | | | | |
| Strong Ale | • | | | | | | | | | | | | | | | | | | | | | | | | |
| **Ciders:** | | | | | | | | | | | | | | | | | | | | | | | | | |
| All types | | | • | | | | | | | | | | | | | | | | | | | | | | |
| **Wines:** | | | | | | | | | | | | | | | | | | | | | | | | | |
| All types | | | | | | | | | • | | | | | | | | | | | | | | | | |
| **Wines, Fortified:** | | | | | | | | | | | | | | | | | | | | | | | | | |
| Port | | | | | | | | | | | | | | | | | • | | | | | | | | |
| Sherry | | | | | | | | | | | | | | | | | • | | | | | | | | |

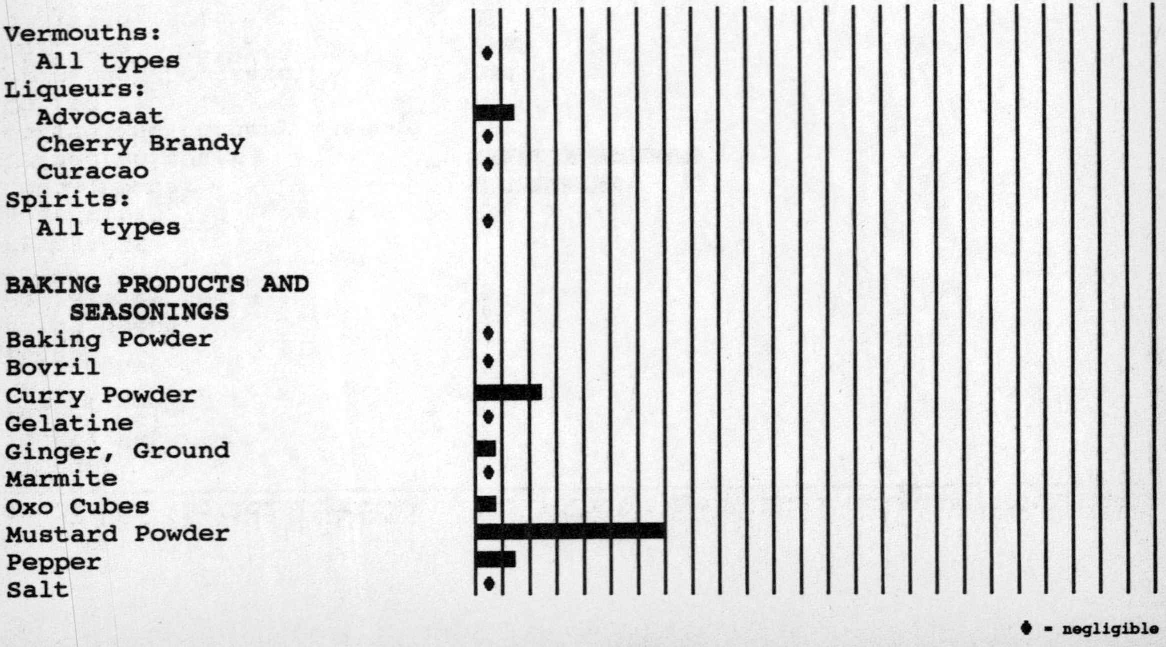

◆ = negligible

Vermouths:
  All types
Liqueurs:
  Advocaat
  Cherry Brandy
  Curacao
Spirits:
  All types

**BAKING PRODUCTS AND SEASONINGS**
  Baking Powder
  Bovril
  Curry Powder
  Gelatine
  Ginger, Ground
  Marmite
  Oxo Cubes
  Mustard Powder
  Pepper
  Salt

## Grams per 25g/1oz (approx)

| Food | Grams |
|---|---|
| Vinegar | • |
| Yeast, Baker's | • |
| Yeast, Dried | 1 |
| **BEANS** | |
| Baked Beans | • |
| Red Kidney Beans | • |
| **BEVERAGES** | |
| Bournvita | 1 |
| Cocoa Powder | 5 |
| Coffee Whitener | 7 |
| Coffee and Chicory Essence | • |
| Coffee | • |
| Drinking Chocolate | 2 |
| Horlicks | 2 |
| Ovaltine | 1 |
| Tea | • |

**BISCUITS - SWEET**
Chocolate, full coated
Cream Biscuits
Digestive, Plain
Digestive, Chocolate
Garibaldi
Ginger Nuts
Jaffa Cakes
Matzo
Muesli Biscuits
Semi-Sweet
Short-Sweet
Shortbread
Wafers, Filled

**BISCUITS - SAVOURY**
Cream Crackers
Crispbread, Rye
Crispbread, Wheat Starch Reduced
Oatcakes

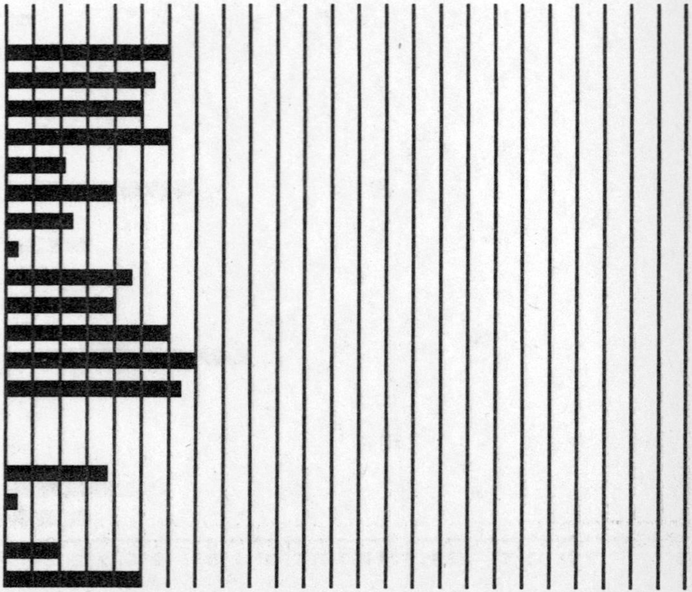

♦ = negligible

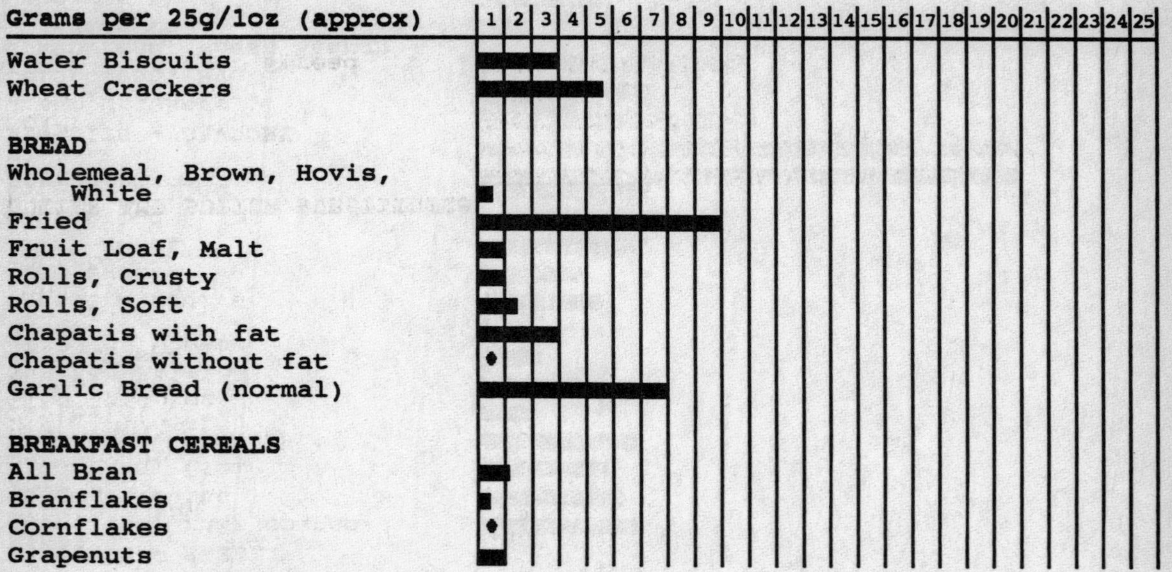

**Grams per 25g/1oz (approx)**

| Food | Grams |
|---|---|
| Water Biscuits | 3 |
| Wheat Crackers | 5 |

**BREAD**

|  |  |
|---|---|
| Wholemeal, Brown, Hovis, White | 1 |
| Fried | 9 |
| Fruit Loaf, Malt | 2 |
| Rolls, Crusty | 2 |
| Rolls, Soft | 2 |
| Chapatis with fat | 3 |
| Chapatis without fat | • |
| Garlic Bread (normal) | 7 |

**BREAKFAST CEREALS**

| Food | Grams |
|---|---|
| All Bran | 2 |
| Branflakes | 1 |
| Cornflakes | • |
| Grapenuts | 2 |

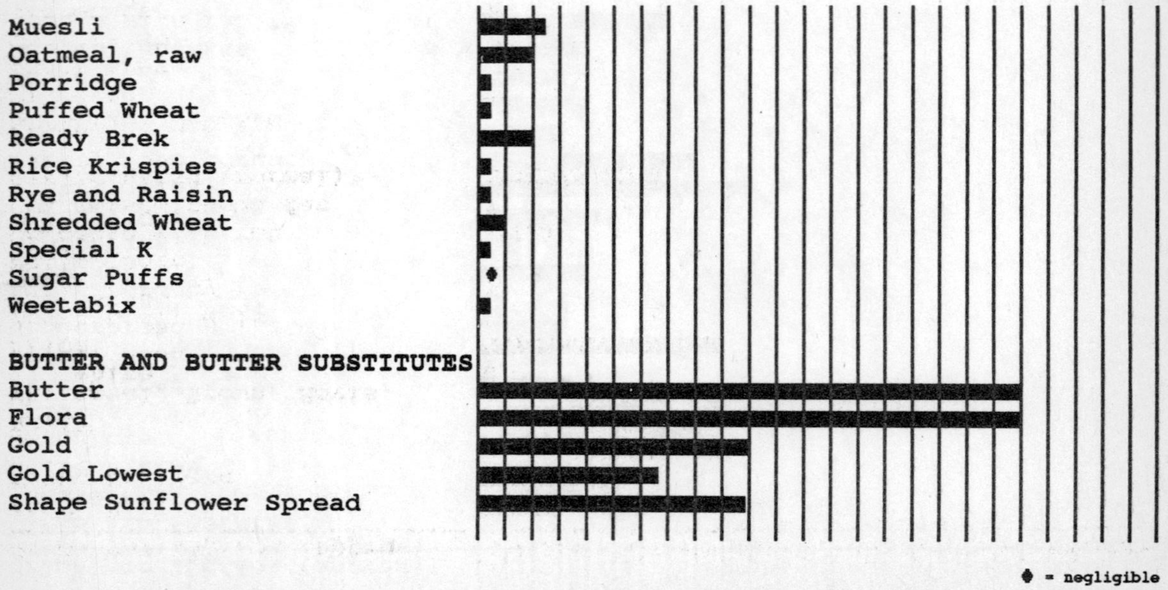

Muesli
Oatmeal, raw
Porridge
Puffed Wheat
Ready Brek
Rice Krispies
Rye and Raisin
Shredded Wheat
Special K
Sugar Puffs
Weetabix

BUTTER AND BUTTER SUBSTITUTES
Butter
Flora
Gold
Gold Lowest
Shape Sunflower Spread

◆ = negligible

| Grams per 25g/1oz (approx) | 1 | 2 | 3 | 4 | 5 | 6 | 7 | 8 | 9 | 10 | 11 | 12 | 13 | 14 | 15 | 16 | 17 | 18 | 19 | 20 | 21 | 22 | 23 | 24 | 25 |
|---|---|---|---|---|---|---|---|---|---|---|---|---|---|---|---|---|---|---|---|---|---|---|---|---|---|
| **CAKES AND PASTRIES** | | | | | | | | | | | | | | | | | | | | | | | | | |
| Cheesecake | | | | 4 | | | | | | | | | | | | | | | | | | | | | |
| Currant Buns | | 2 | | | | | | | | | | | | | | | | | | | | | | | |
| Doughnuts | | | | 4 | | | | | | | | | | | | | | | | | | | | | |
| Eclairs | | | | | | 6 | | | | | | | | | | | | | | | | | | | |
| Fancy, Iced | | | 3 | | | | | | | | | | | | | | | | | | | | | | |
| Fruit, Rich | | | 3 | | | | | | | | | | | | | | | | | | | | | | |
| Gingerbread | | | 3 | | | | | | | | | | | | | | | | | | | | | | |
| Jam Tarts | 1 | | | | | | | | | | | | | | | | | | | | | | | | |
| Madeira | | | 3 | | | | | | | | | | | | | | | | | | | | | | |
| Mince Pies | | 2 | | | | | | | | | | | | | | | | | | | | | | | |
| Pastry, Choux | | | | 4 | | | | | | | | | | | | | | | | | | | | | |
| Pastry, Flaky | | | | | | | | | | 10 | | | | | | | | | | | | | | | |
| Pastry, Shortcrust | | | | | | | | 8 | | | | | | | | | | | | | | | | | |
| Plain | | | 3 | | | | | | | | | | | | | | | | | | | | | | |
| Rock | | | 3 | | | | | | | | | | | | | | | | | | | | | | |
| Scones | | | 3 | | | | | | | | | | | | | | | | | | | | | | |
| Scotch Pancakes | | | | 4 | | | | | | | | | | | | | | | | | | | | | |
| Sponge with fat | | | | | | | 7 | | | | | | | | | | | | | | | | | | |

Sponge without fat

**CHEESE**
Shape Brie
Camembert
Cheddar
Shape White and Coloured Cheddar
Shape Mature Cheddar
Ordinary Mature Cheddar
Vegetarian Cheddar
Shape Cheshire
Ordinary Cheshire
Danish Blue
Edam
Shape Edam
Double Gloucester
Gouda
Gruyere
Red Leicester
Lymeswold

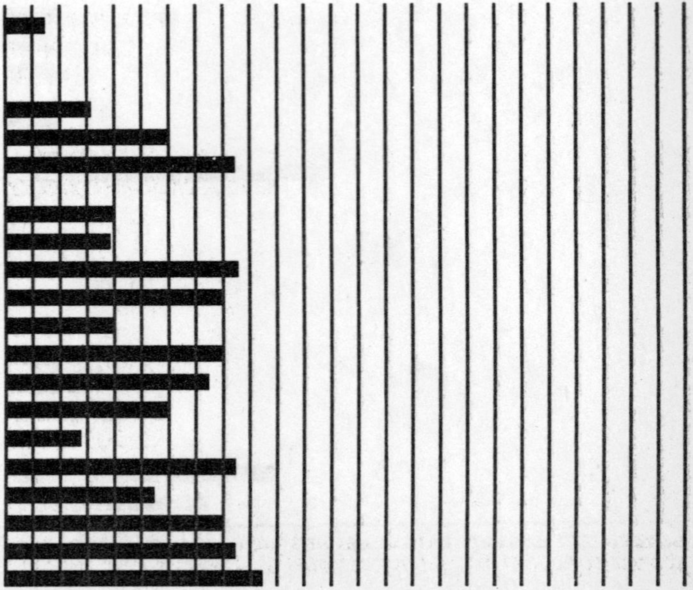

♦ = negligible

| Grams per 25g/1oz (approx) | 1 | 2 | 3 | 4 | 5 | 6 | 7 | 8 | 9 | 10 | 11 | 12 | 13 | 14 | 15 | 16 | 17 | 18 | 19 | 20 | 21 | 22 | 23 | 24 | 25 |
|---|---|---|---|---|---|---|---|---|---|---|---|---|---|---|---|---|---|---|---|---|---|---|---|---|---|
| Parmesan | | | | | | | 7 | | | | | | | | | | | | | | | | | | |
| Stilton | | | | | | | | | 9 | | | | | | | | | | | | | | | | |
| Cottage with Cream | 1 | | | | | | | | | | | | | | | | | | | | | | | | |
| Cottage without Cream | • | | | | | | | | | | | | | | | | | | | | | | | | |
| Shape Cottage Cheese – Plain | 1 | | | | | | | | | | | | | | | | | | | | | | | | |
| Shape Cottage Cheeses: | | | | | | | | | | | | | | | | | | | | | | | | | |
|   Cottage Cheese with Pineapple | 1 | | | | | | | | | | | | | | | | | | | | | | | | |
|   with Onion and Chives | 1 | | | | | | | | | | | | | | | | | | | | | | | | |
|   with Caribbean Fruit | 1 | | | | | | | | | | | | | | | | | | | | | | | | |
|   Mexican Style | 1 | | | | | | | | | | | | | | | | | | | | | | | | |
|   Italian Style | 1 | | | | | | | | | | | | | | | | | | | | | | | | |
| Cream Cheese | | | | | | | | | | | 11 | | | | | | | | | | | | | | |
| Shape Soft Cheeses: | | | | | | | | | | | | | | | | | | | | | | | | | |
|   Low Fat Soft Cheese | 2 | | | | | | | | | | | | | | | | | | | | | | | | |
|   Low Fat Soft Cheese with Garlic and Herbs | 2 | | | | | | | | | | | | | | | | | | | | | | | | |
|   with Onion and Chives | 2 | | | | | | | | | | | | | | | | | | | | | | | | |
|   with Orange | 2 | | | | | | | | | | | | | | | | | | | | | | | | |

|  |  |
| --- | --- |
| with Pineapple | |
| with Walnut | |
| with Smoked Ham | |
| with Natural Blue Cheese | |
| with Natural Cheddar | |
| Cheese Spread | |
| | |
| **CONDIMENTS** | |
| Apple Sauce | |
| Cranberry Sauce | ♦ |
| English Mustard | ♦ |
| Horseradish Sauce | |
| Redcurrant Jelly | ♦ |
| Tartare Sauce | |
| | |
| **CONFECTIONERY** | |
| Boiled Sweets | ♦ |
| Chocolate, average, Milk or Plain | |
| Chocolate, Fancy and Filled | |
| Chocolate - Nut and Raisin | |

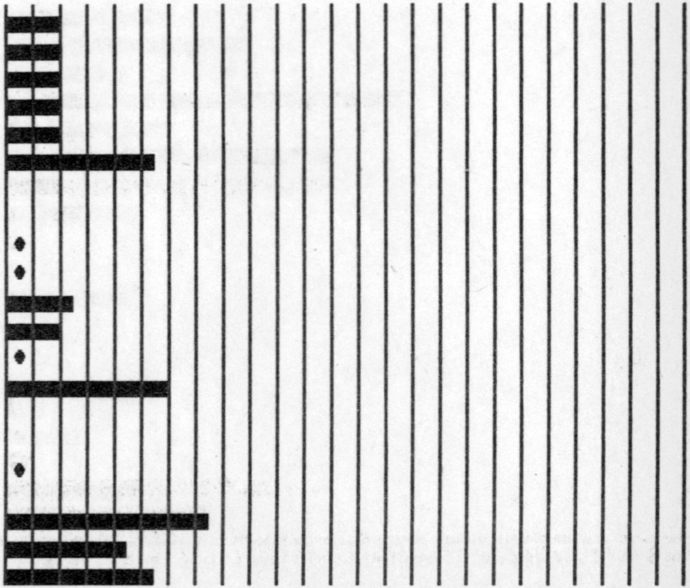

♦ = negligible

| Grams per 25g/1oz (approx)   | 1 | 2 | 3 | 4 | 5 | 6 | 7 | 8 | 9 | 10 | 11 | 12 | 13 | 14 | 15 | 16 | 17 | 18 | 19 | 20 | 21 | 22 | 23 | 24 | 25 |
|---|---|---|---|---|---|---|---|---|---|---|---|---|---|---|---|---|---|---|---|---|---|---|---|---|---|
| Bounty Bar | | | | | | 7 | | | | | | | | | | | | | | | | | | | |
| Mars Bar | | | | | 5 | | | | | | | | | | | | | | | | | | | | |
| Fruit Gums | ● | | | | | | | | | | | | | | | | | | | | | | | | |
| Fudge | | | 3 | | | | | | | | | | | | | | | | | | | | | | |
| Humbugs | | 2 | | | | | | | | | | | | | | | | | | | | | | | |
| Liquorice | ● | | | | | | | | | | | | | | | | | | | | | | | | |
| Pastilles | ● ● | | | | | | | | | | | | | | | | | | | | | | | | |
| Peppermints | | | | | | | | | | | | | | | | | | | | | | | | | |
| Toffees | | | | | 5 | | | | | | | | | | | | | | | | | | | | |
| | | | | | | | | | | | | | | | | | | | | | | | | | |
| CREAM AND CREAM SUBSTITUTES | | | | | | | | | | | | | | | | | | | | | | | | | |
| Cream, single | | | | | 5 | | | | | | | | | | | | | | | | | | | | |
| Shape, single | | | 3 | | | | | | | | | | | | | | | | | | | | | | |
| Cream, Double | | | | | | | | | | | 12 | | | | | | | | | | | | | | |
| Shape, Double | | | | | | 6 | | | | | | | | | | | | | | | | | | | |
| Cream, Cornish Clotted | | | | | | | | | | | | | | | 15 | | | | | | | | | | |
| Cream, Soured | | | | | 5 | | | | | | | | | | | | | | | | | | | | |
| Cream, Whipping | | | | | | | | | 9 | | | | | | | | | | | | | | | | |
| Cream, Sterilised Canned | | | | | | 6 | | | | | | | | | | | | | | | | | | | |

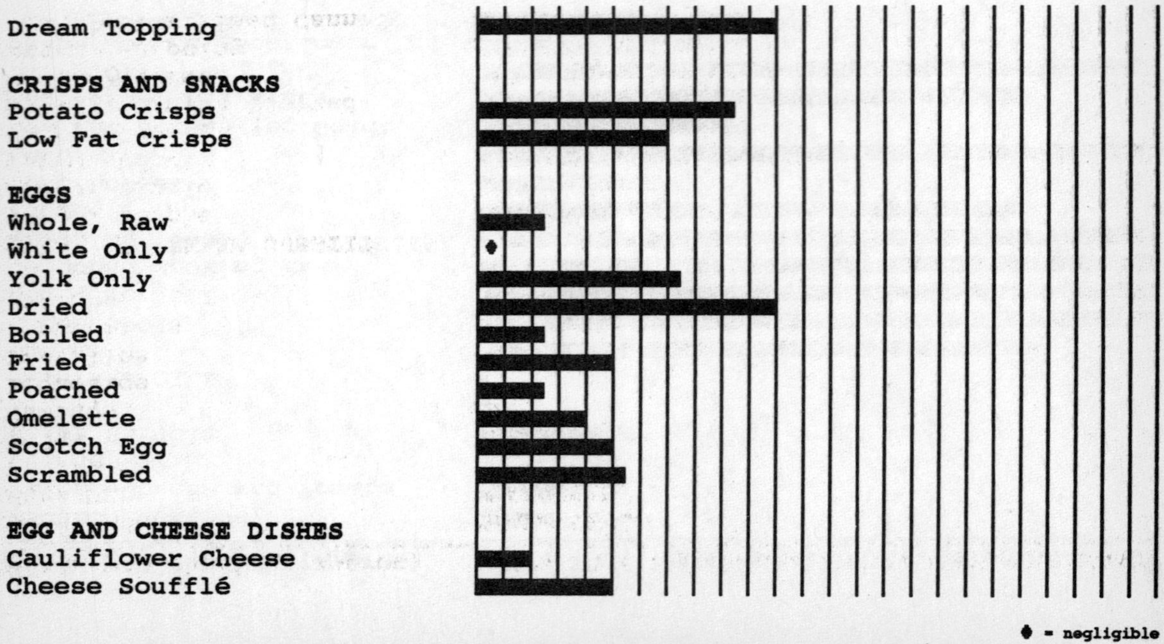

Dream Topping

## CRISPS AND SNACKS
Potato Crisps
Low Fat Crisps

## EGGS
Whole, Raw
White Only
Yolk Only
Dried
Boiled
Fried
Poached
Omelette
Scotch Egg
Scrambled

## EGG AND CHEESE DISHES
Cauliflower Cheese
Cheese Soufflé

♦ = negligible

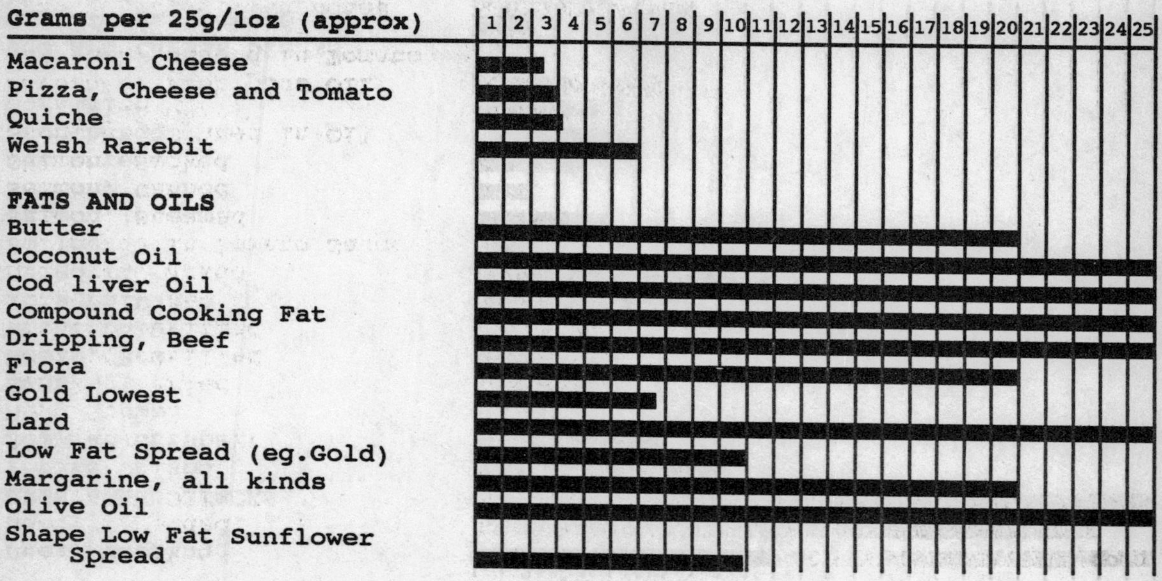

## Grams per 25g/1oz (approx)

| Food | Grams |
|---|---|
| Macaroni Cheese | 2 |
| Pizza, Cheese and Tomato | 3 |
| Quiche | 3 |
| Welsh Rarebit | 5 |

### FATS AND OILS

| Food | Grams |
|---|---|
| Butter | 19 |
| Coconut Oil | 25 |
| Cod liver Oil | 25 |
| Compound Cooking Fat | 25 |
| Dripping, Beef | 25 |
| Flora | 19 |
| Gold Lowest | 7 |
| Lard | 25 |
| Low Fat Spread (eg. Gold) | 10 |
| Margarine, all kinds | 19 |
| Olive Oil | 25 |
| Shape Low Fat Sunflower Spread | 9 |

Suet, Block
Suet, Shredded
Vegetable Oils

**FISH - Fatty Fish**
Eel, Stewed
Herring, Fried
Herring, Grilled
Bloater, Grilled
Kipper, Baked
Mackerel, Fried
Pilchards in Tomato Sauce
Salmon, Steamed
Salmon, Canned
Salmon, Smoked
Sardines, Canned in Oil
  (fish only)
Sardines, Fish plus Oil
Sardines, Canned in Tomato
  Sauce
Sprats, Fried with Bones

♦ = negligible

**Grams per 25g/1oz (approx)**

| | 1 2 3 4 5 6 7 8 9 10 11 12 13 14 15 16 17 18 19 20 21 22 23 24 25 |
|---|---|
| Trout, (Brown) Steamed with Bones | |
| Tuna | |
| Whitebait, Fried | |
| | |
| **FISH - White Fish** | |
| Cod, Baked | |
| Cod, Fried in Batter | |
| Cod, Grilled | |
| Cod, Poached | |
| Cod, Steamed | |
| Cod, Smoked, Poached | |
| Haddock, Fried | |
| Haddock, Steamed | |
| Haddock, Smoked, Steamed | |
| Halibut, Steamed | |
| Lemon Sole, Fried | |
| Lemon Sole, Steamed | |
| Plaice, Fried in Batter | |

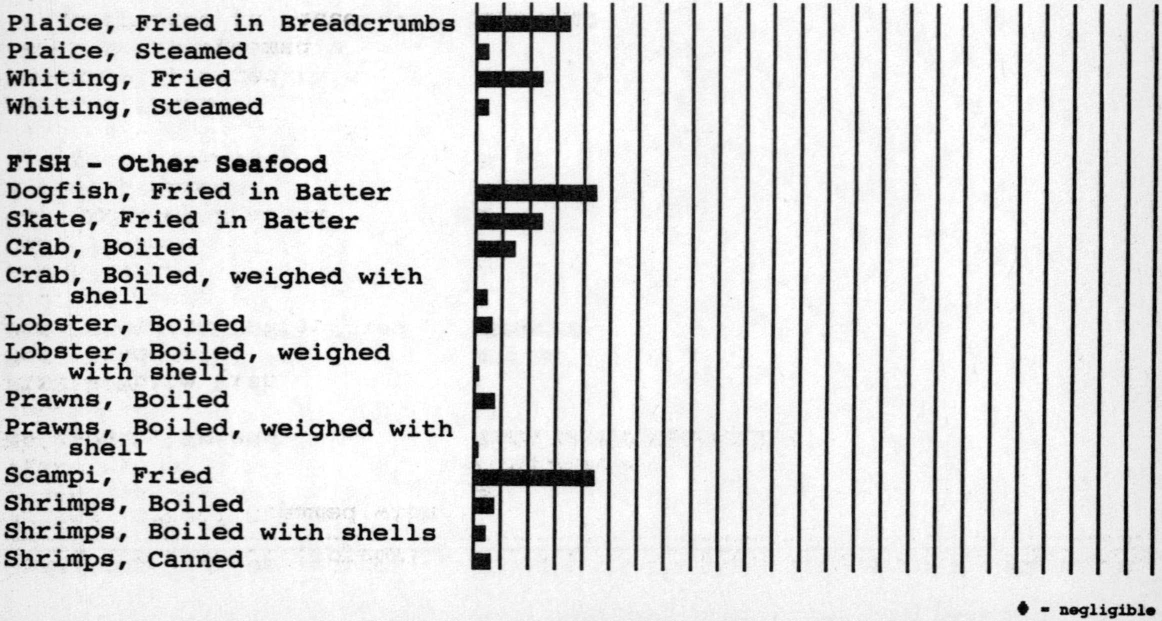

Plaice, Fried in Breadcrumbs
Plaice, steamed
Whiting, Fried
Whiting, Steamed

**FISH – Other Seafood**
Dogfish, Fried in Batter
Skate, Fried in Batter
Crab, Boiled
Crab, Boiled, weighed with shell
Lobster, Boiled
Lobster, Boiled, weighed with shell
Prawns, Boiled
Prawns, Boiled, weighed with shell
Scampi, Fried
Shrimps, Boiled
Shrimps, Boiled with shells
Shrimps, Canned

♦ = negligible

## Grams per 25g/1oz (approx)

| | 1 | 2 | 3 | 4 | 5 | 6 | 7 | 8 | 9 | 10 | 11 | 12 | 13 | 14 | 15 | 16 | 17 | 18 | 19 | 20 | 21 | 22 | 23 | 24 | 25 |
|---|---|---|---|---|---|---|---|---|---|---|---|---|---|---|---|---|---|---|---|---|---|---|---|---|---|
| Cockles, Boiled | | | | | | | | | | | | | | | | | | | | | | | | | |
| Mussels, Boiled | | | | | | | | | | | | | | | | | | | | | | | | | |
| Oysters, Raw | | | | | | | | | | | | | | | | | | | | | | | | | |
| Scallops, Steamed | | | | | | | | | | | | | | | | | | | | | | | | | |
| Whelks, Boiled | | | | | | | | | | | | | | | | | | | | | | | | | |
| Winkles | | | | | | | | | | | | | | | | | | | | | | | | | |
| Roe, (cod hard) Fried | | | | | | | | | | | | | | | | | | | | | | | | | |
| Roe, (herring soft) Fried | | | | | | | | | | | | | | | | | | | | | | | | | |

### FLOUR
Cornflour
Custard Powder
Flour, Wholemeal
Flour, White, etc.

### FROMAGE FRAIS
Ordinary Fromage Frais
Low Fat Fromage Frais
Shape Apricot Fromage Frais

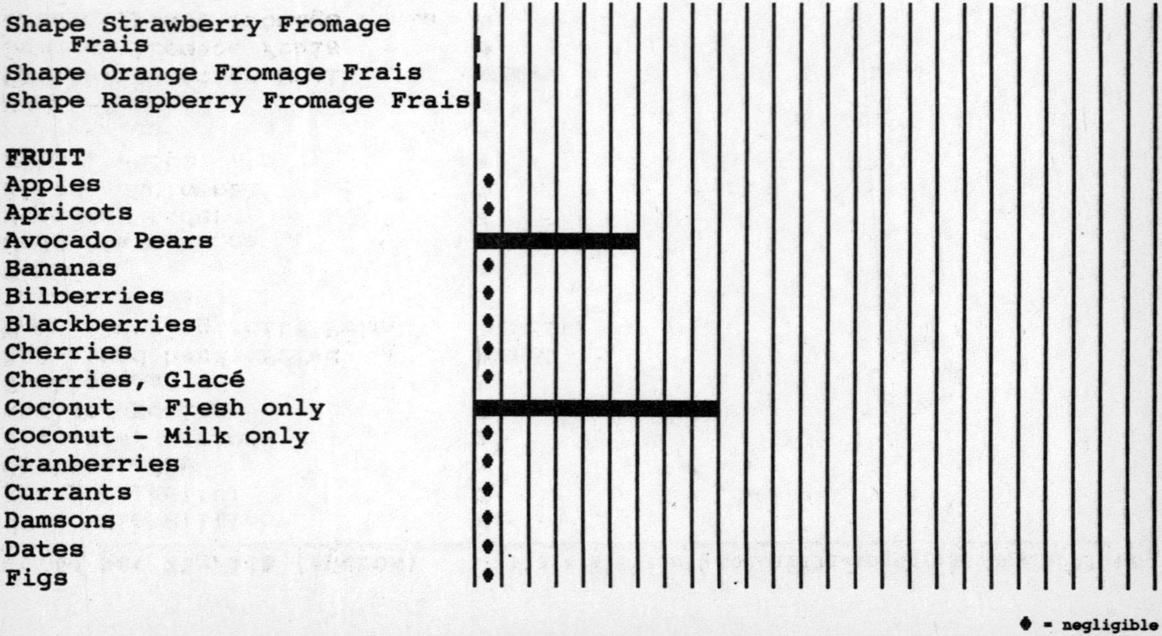

Shape Strawberry Fromage Frais
Shape Orange Fromage Frais
Shape Raspberry Fromage Frais

**FRUIT**
Apples
Apricots
Avocado Pears
Bananas
Bilberries
Blackberries
Cherries
Cherries, Glacé
Coconut – Flesh only
Coconut – Milk only
Cranberries
Currants
Damsons
Dates
Figs

♦ = negligible

| Grams per 25g/1oz (approx) | 1 | 2 | 3 | 4 | 5 | 6 | 7 | 8 | 9 | 10 | 11 | 12 | 13 | 14 | 15 | 16 | 17 | 18 | 19 | 20 | 21 | 22 | 23 | 24 | 25 |
|---|---|---|---|---|---|---|---|---|---|---|---|---|---|---|---|---|---|---|---|---|---|---|---|---|---|
| Fruit Pie Filling | ♦ | | | | | | | | | | | | | | | | | | | | | | | | |
| Fruit Salad | ♦ | | | | | | | | | | | | | | | | | | | | | | | | |
| Gooseberries | ♦ | | | | | | | | | | | | | | | | | | | | | | | | |
| Grapes | ♦ | | | | | | | | | | | | | | | | | | | | | | | | |
| Grapefruit | ♦ | | | | | | | | | | | | | | | | | | | | | | | | |
| Greengages | ♦ | | | | | | | | | | | | | | | | | | | | | | | | |
| Guavas | ♦ | | | | | | | | | | | | | | | | | | | | | | | | |
| Lemons | ♦ | | | | | | | | | | | | | | | | | | | | | | | | |
| Loganberries | ♦ | | | | | | | | | | | | | | | | | | | | | | | | |
| Lychees | ♦ | | | | | | | | | | | | | | | | | | | | | | | | |
| Mandarin Oranges | ♦ | | | | | | | | | | | | | | | | | | | | | | | | |
| Mangoes | ♦ | | | | | | | | | | | | | | | | | | | | | | | | |
| Medlars | ♦ | | | | | | | | | | | | | | | | | | | | | | | | |
| Melons | ♦ | | | | | | | | | | | | | | | | | | | | | | | | |
| Mulberries | ♦ | | | | | | | | | | | | | | | | | | | | | | | | |
| Nectarines | ♦ | | | | | | | | | | | | | | | | | | | | | | | | |
| Olives | ███ | | | | | | | | | | | | | | | | | | | | | | | | |
| Oranges | ♦ | | | | | | | | | | | | | | | | | | | | | | | | |
| Passion Fruit | ♦ | | | | | | | | | | | | | | | | | | | | | | | | |

Paw Paw
Peaches
Pears
Pineapple
Plums
Pomegranate
Prunes
Quinces
Raisins
Raspberries
Rhubarb
Strawberries
Sultanas
Tangerines

**GAME**
Grouse, Roast, weighed with bone
Partridge:
 Roast
 Roast, weighed with bone

♦ = negligible

| Grams per 25g/1oz (approx) | 1 2 3 4 5 6 7 8 9 10 11 12 13 14 15 16 17 18 19 20 21 22 23 24 25 |
|---|---|
| **Pheasant:** | |
| Roast | |
| Roast, weighed with bone | |
| **Pigeon:** | |
| Roast | |
| Roast, weighed with bone | |
| **Hare:** | |
| Stewed | |
| Stewed weighed with bone | |
| **Rabbit:** | |
| Stewed | |
| Stewed weighed with bone | |
| Venison, Roast | |

**GRAINS**
Barley, Pearl
Bran
Rye
Sago

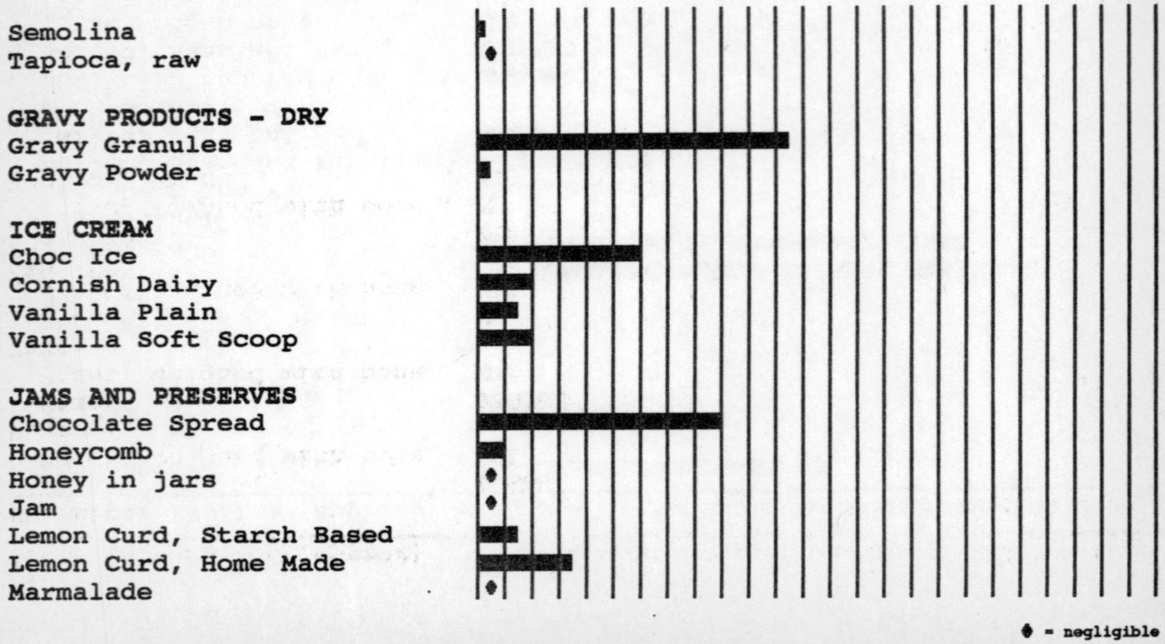

Semolina
Tapioca, raw

**GRAVY PRODUCTS - DRY**
Gravy Granules
Gravy Powder

**ICE CREAM**
Choc Ice
Cornish Dairy
Vanilla Plain
Vanilla Soft Scoop

**JAMS AND PRESERVES**
Chocolate Spread
Honeycomb
Honey in jars
Jam
Lemon Curd, Starch Based
Lemon Curd, Home Made
Marmalade

♦ = negligible

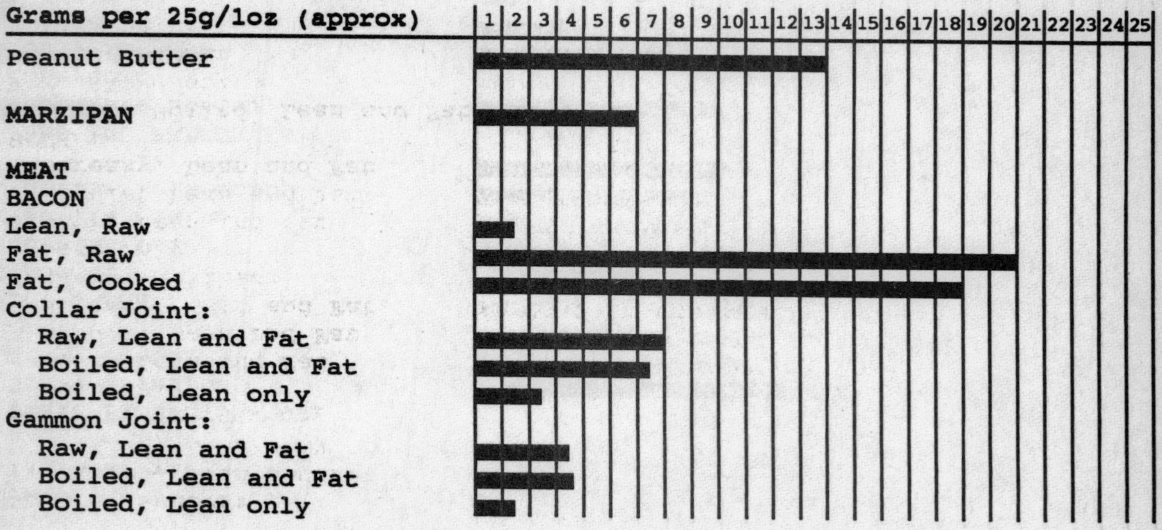

## Grams per 25g/1oz (approx)

|  |  |
|---|---|
| Peanut Butter | 13 |
| MARZIPAN | 6 |
| **MEAT** | |
| **BACON** | |
| Lean, Raw | 1 |
| Fat, Raw | 20 |
| Fat, Cooked | 18 |
| Collar Joint: | |
|   Raw, Lean and Fat | 7 |
|   Boiled, Lean and Fat | 7 |
|   Boiled, Lean only | 3 |
| Gammon Joint: | |
|   Raw, Lean and Fat | 4 |
|   Boiled, Lean and Fat | 4 |
|   Boiled, Lean only | 1 |

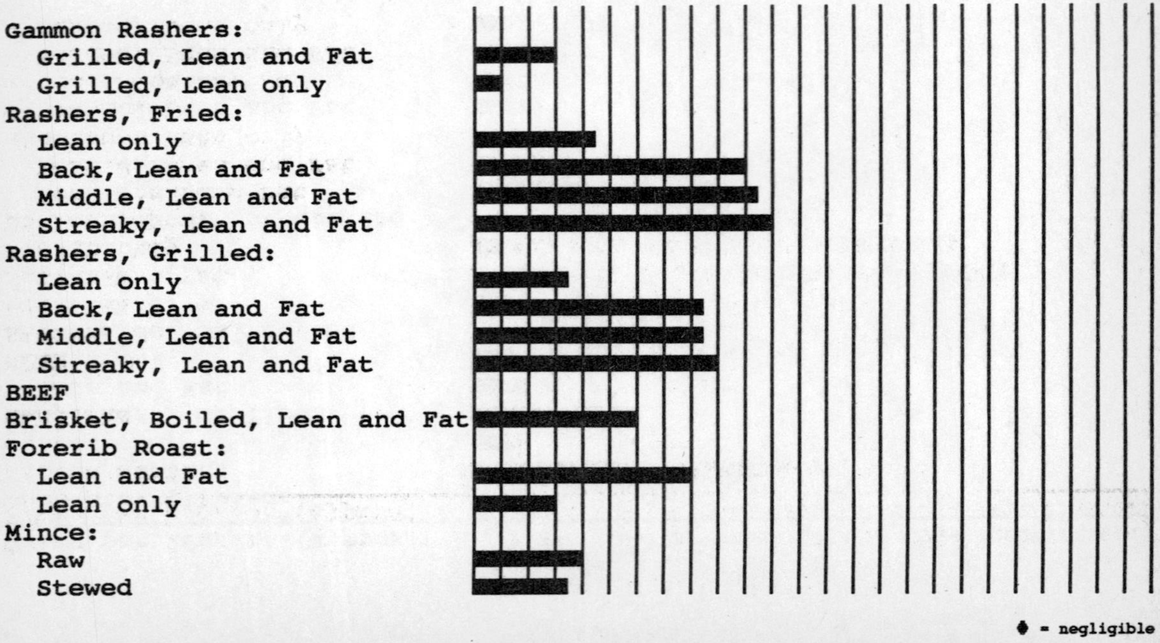

```
Gammon Rashers:
  Grilled, Lean and Fat
  Grilled, Lean only
Rashers, Fried:
  Lean only
  Back, Lean and Fat
  Middle, Lean and Fat
  Streaky, Lean and Fat
Rashers, Grilled:
  Lean only
  Back, Lean and Fat
  Middle, Lean and Fat
  Streaky, Lean and Fat
BEEF
Brisket, Boiled, Lean and Fat
Forerib Roast:
  Lean and Fat
  Lean only
Mince:
  Raw
  Stewed
```

♦ = negligible

## Grams per 25g/1oz (approx)

| | 1 2 3 4 5 6 7 8 9 10 11 12 13 14 15 16 17 18 19 20 21 22 23 24 25 |
|---|---|
| Rump Steak, Fried: | |
|   Lean and Fat | 4 |
|   Lean only | 2 |
| Rump Steak, Grilled: | |
|   Lean and Fat | 4 |
|   Lean only | 2 |
| Silverside, Salted and Boiled: | |
|   Lean and Fat | 4 |
|   Lean only | 1 |
| Sirloin, Roast or Grilled: | |
|   Lean and Fat | 5 |
|   Lean only | 2 |
| Stewing Steak: | |
|   Stewed, Lean and Fat | 2 |
| Topside Roast: | |
|   Lean and Fat | 3 |
|   Lean only | 1 |

## LAMB

Breast, Roast:
    Lean and Fat
    Lean only

Chops, Loin, Grilled:
    Lean and Fat
    Lean and Fat weighed with bone
    Lean only
    Lean only weighed with bone

Cutlets, Grilled:
    Lean and Fat
    Lean and Fat weighed with bone
    Lean only
    Lean only weighed with bone

Leg Roast:
    Lean and Fat
    Lean only

♦ = negligible

## Grams per 25g/1oz (approx)

| Item | Grams |
|---|---|
| **Scrag and Neck, Stewed:** | |
| Lean and Fat | 5 |
| Lean only | 3 |
| Lean only weighed with bone | 2 |
| **Shoulder Roast:** | |
| Lean and Fat | 6 |
| Lean only | 3 |
| **PORK** | |
| **Belly Rashers:** | |
| Grilled Lean and Fat | 8 |
| **Chops, Loin, Grilled:** | |
| Lean and Fat | 6 |
| Lean and Fat weighed with bone | 4 |
| Lean only | 2 |
| Lean only weighed with fat and bone | 1 |

Leg Roast:
  Lean and Fat
  Lean only
VEAL
Cutlet, Fried
Fillet, Roast

MEATS CANNED
Corned Beef
Ham
Ham and Pork, Chopped
Luncheon Meat
Stewed Steak with Gravy
Tongue
Veal, Jellied

MEAT - COOKED DISHES
Beef Steak Pudding
Beef Stew
Bolognese Sauce
Curried Meat

◆ = negligible

**Grams per 25g/1oz (approx)**

| Food | Grams |
|---|---|
| Hot Pot | 1 |
| Irish Stew | 2 |
| Moussaka | 4 |
| Shepherds Pie | 2 |

**MEAT PRODUCTS**

| Food | Grams |
|---|---|
| Beefburgers, Fried | 5 |
| Black Pudding, Fried | 6 |
| Brawn | 3 |
| Chicken Roll | 2 |
| Faggots | 5 |
| Frankfurters | 6 |
| Haggis, Boiled | 5 |
| Liver Sausage | 7 |
| Meat Paste | 3 |
| Polony | 5 |
| Salami | 9 |

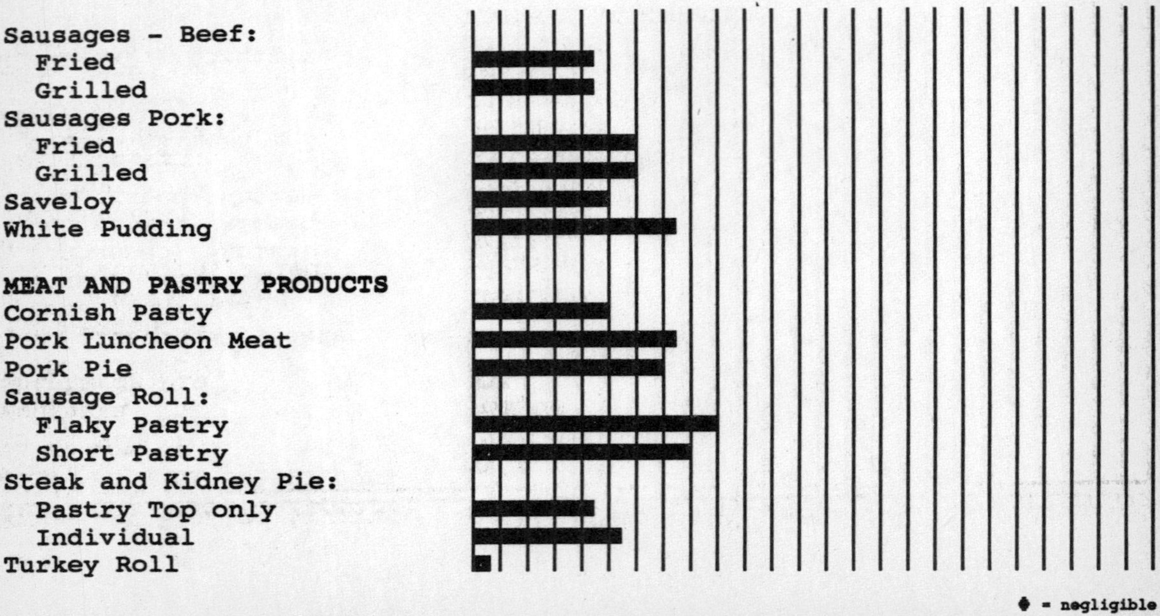

Sausages - Beef:
    Fried
    Grilled
Sausages Pork:
    Fried
    Grilled
Saveloy
White Pudding

**MEAT AND PASTRY PRODUCTS**
Cornish Pasty
Pork Luncheon Meat
Pork Pie
Sausage Roll:
    Flaky Pastry
    Short Pastry
Steak and Kidney Pie:
    Pastry Top only
    Individual
Turkey Roll

♦ = negligible

Grams per 25g/1oz (approx) | 1 2 3 4 5 6 7 8 9 10 11 12 13 14 15 16 17 18 19 20 21 22 23 24 25

## MILK AND MILK SUBSTITUTES

Milk, Cow's:
- Fresh, Whole
- Channel Isles
- Sterilised
- Longlife, UHT Treated
- Fresh, Skimmed
- Shape – semi skimmed
- Condensed, Whole
- Condensed, Skimmed
- Evaporated, Whole
- Dried, Whole
- Dried, Skimmed
- Milk, Goats

MINCEMEAT – (fruit)

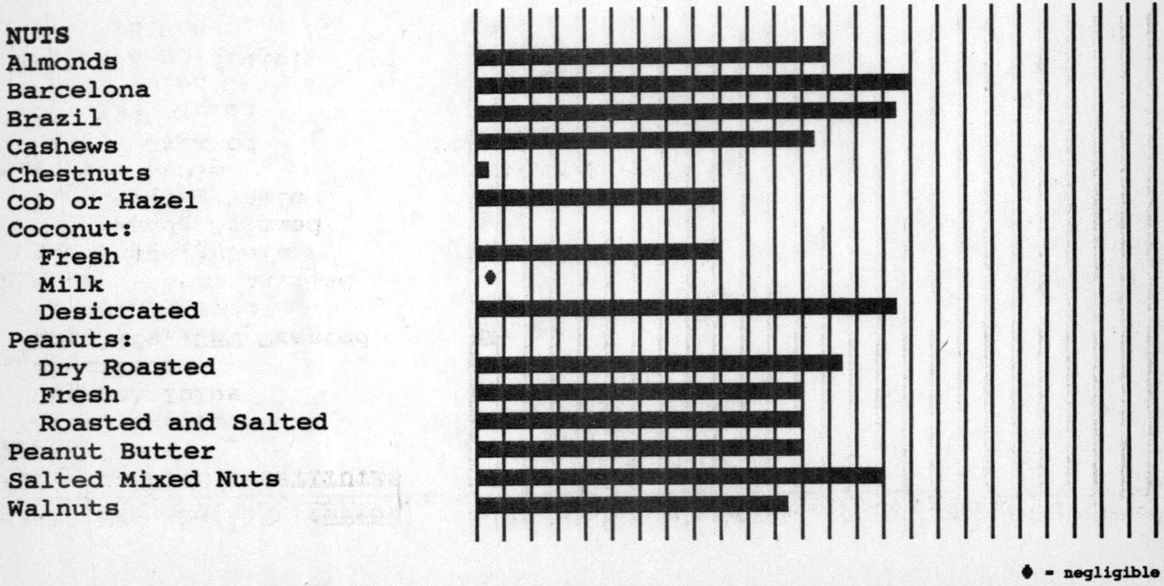

NUTS
Almonds
Barcelona
Brazil
Cashews
Chestnuts
Cob or Hazel
Coconut:
　Fresh
　Milk
　Desiccated
Peanuts:
　Dry Roasted
　Fresh
　Roasted and Salted
Peanut Butter
Salted Mixed Nuts
Walnuts

♦ = negligible

## Grams per 25g/1oz (approx)

**OFFAL**

Brain:
- Calf, Boiled
- Lamb, Boiled

Heart:
- Sheep, Roast
- Ox, Stewed

Kidney:
- Lamb, Fried
- Ox, Stewed
- Pig, Stewed

Liver:
- Calf, Fried
- Chicken, Fried
- Lamb, Fried
- Ox, Stewed
- Pig, Stewed

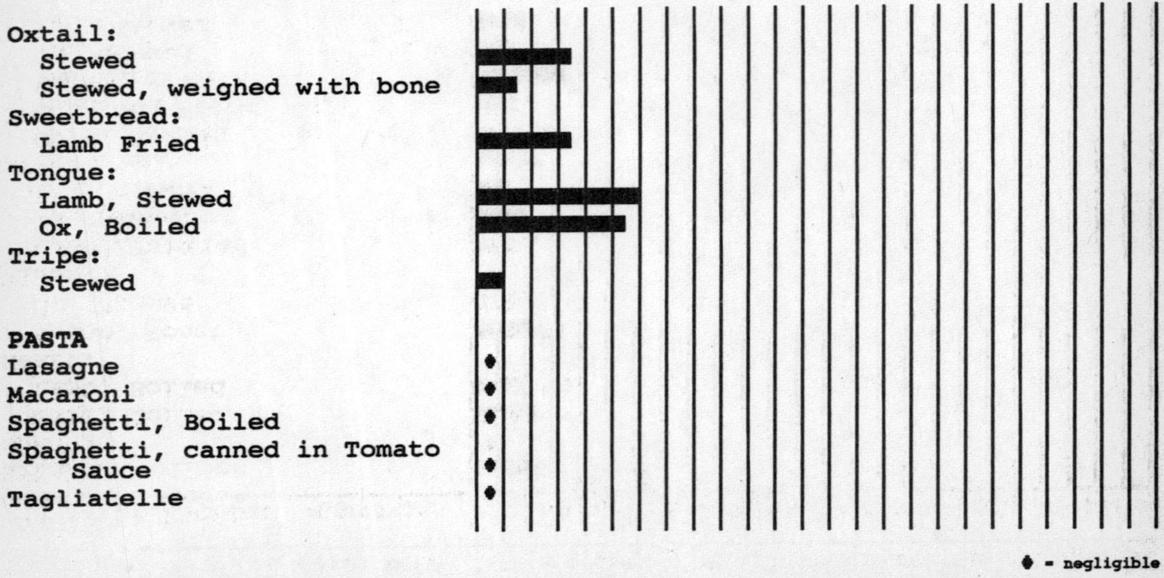

## Oxtail:
Stewed
Stewed, weighed with bone

## Sweetbread:
Lamb Fried

## Tongue:
Lamb, Stewed
Ox, Boiled

## Tripe:
Stewed

## PASTA
Lasagne
Macaroni
Spaghetti, Boiled
Spaghetti, canned in Tomato Sauce
Tagliatelle

♦ = negligible

| Grams per 25g/1oz (approx) | 1 2 3 4 5 6 7 8 9 10 11 12 13 14 15 16 17 18 19 20 21 22 23 24 25 |

**PICKLES**
Branston Pickle
Cocktail Olives
Chutney
Piccalilli
Pickle, Sweet

**PIZZA**

**POULTRY**
Chicken, Boiled:
  Meat only
  Light Meat
  Dark Meat
Chicken Roast:
  Meat only
  Meat and Skin
  Light Meat
  Dark Meat

Wing Quarter, weighed with
  bone
Leg Quarter, weighed with
  bone
Duck Roast:
  Meat only
  Meat, Fat and Skin
Goose, Roast
Turkey Roast:
  Meat only
  Meat and Skin
  Light Meat
  Dark Meat

PUDDINGS
Angel Delight (made up)
Apple Crumble
Bread and Butter Pudding
Cheesecake
Christmas Pudding
Egg Custard

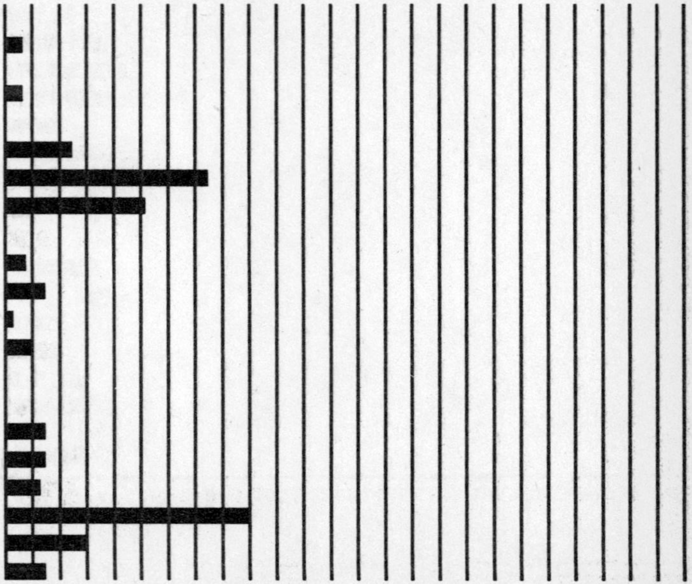

♦ = negligible

| Grams per 25g/1oz (approx) | 1 | 2 | 3 | 4 | 5 | 6 | 7 | 8 | 9 | 10 | 11 | 12 | 13 | 14 | 15 | 16 | 17 | 18 | 19 | 20 | 21 | 22 | 23 | 24 | 25 |
|---|---|---|---|---|---|---|---|---|---|---|---|---|---|---|---|---|---|---|---|---|---|---|---|---|---|
| Dumpling | | | 3 | | | | | | | | | | | | | | | | | | | | | | |
| Fruit Pie with Pastry Top and Bottom | | | | 4 | | | | | | | | | | | | | | | | | | | | | |
| Fruit Pie Pastry Top Only | | 1½ | | | | | | | | | | | | | | | | | | | | | | | |
| Ice-Cream, Dairy | | 2 | | | | | | | | | | | | | | | | | | | | | | | |
| Ice-Cream, non Dairy | | 2 | | | | | | | | | | | | | | | | | | | | | | | |
| Jelly | ● | | | | | | | | | | | | | | | | | | | | | | | | |
| Lemon Meringue Pie | | | | 3½ | | | | | | | | | | | | | | | | | | | | | |
| Meringues | ● | | | | | | | | | | | | | | | | | | | | | | | | |
| Milk Puddings | 1 | | | | | | | | | | | | | | | | | | | | | | | | |
| Rice, Canned | ½ | | | | | | | | | | | | | | | | | | | | | | | | |
| Pancakes | | | | 4 | | | | | | | | | | | | | | | | | | | | | |
| Queen of Puddings | | 2 | | | | | | | | | | | | | | | | | | | | | | | |
| Sponge Pudding | | | | 4 | | | | | | | | | | | | | | | | | | | | | |
| Suet Pudding | | | | | 4½ | | | | | | | | | | | | | | | | | | | | |
| Treacle Tart | | | | 3½ | | | | | | | | | | | | | | | | | | | | | |
| Trifle | | 1½ | | | | | | | | | | | | | | | | | | | | | | | |

**PULSES AND LENTILS - Cooked**
Black Eye Beans
Butter Beans
Chick Peas
Continental Lentils
Green Split Peas
Haricot Beans
Lentils
Mung Beans
Red Kidney Beans
Yellow Split Peas

**QUICHE LORRAINE**

**RICE**
Cooked
Savoury - Dry Weight

**SALAD PRODUCTS**
Coleslaw, Low Calorie
Coleslaw, Normal

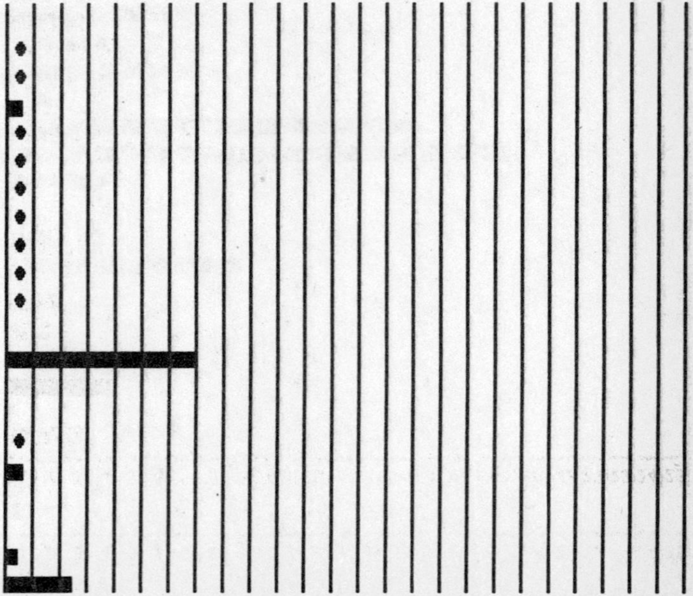

♦ = negligible

## Grams per 25g/1oz (approx)

| Item | Grams |
|---|---|
| Shape Coleslaw | ~1 |
| Shape 1000 Island Coleslaw | ~1 |
| Shape Garlic and Herb Coleslaw | ~1 |
| Shape Potato Salad | ~1 |
| Shape Curried Potato Salad | ~1 |
| Shape Chilli Potato Salad | ~1 |
| **SAUCES** | |
| 1000 Island Dressing | 9 |
| Bread Sauce | 2 |
| Brown Sauce | <1 |
| Cheese Sauce | 4 |
| French Dressing | 18 |
| Mayonnaise | 15 |
| Onion Sauce | 2 |
| Salad Cream | 7 |
| Waistline | 3 |
| Seafood Dressing - non diet | 7 |

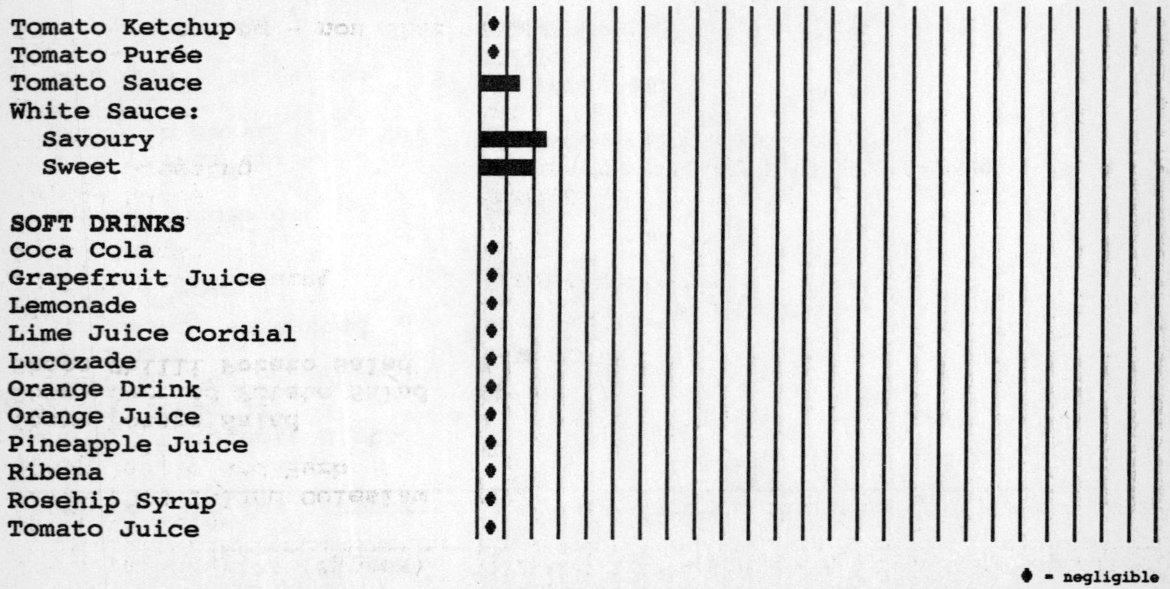

Tomato Ketchup
Tomato Purée
Tomato Sauce
White Sauce:
    Savoury
    Sweet

**SOFT DRINKS**
Coca Cola
Grapefruit Juice
Lemonade
Lime Juice Cordial
Lucozade
Orange Drink
Orange Juice
Pineapple Juice
Ribena
Rosehip Syrup
Tomato Juice

♦ = negligible

| Grams per 25g/1oz (approx) | 1 2 3 4 5 6 7 8 9 10 11 12 13 14 15 16 17 18 19 20 21 22 23 24 25 |
|---|---|
| **SOUPS** | |
| Bone and Vegetable Broth | |
| Chicken Cream of: | |
|   Ready to Serve | |
|   Condensed | |
|   Condensed, as Served | |
| Chicken Noodle | |
| Lentil | |
| Minestrone | |
| Mushroom, Cream of | |
| Oxtail | |
| Tomato, Cream of: | |
|   Ready to Serve | |
|   Condensed | |
|   Condensed, as Served | |
| Vegetable | |

**SOYA**
Soya, full fat
Soya, low fat

**SUGARS**
Glucose Liquid
Sugar, all
Syrup
Treacle

**VEGETABLES**
Ackee, Canned
Artichokes:
  Globe, Boiled
  Jerusalem, Boiled
Asparagus
Aubergine
Avocado
Beans:
  French
  Runner

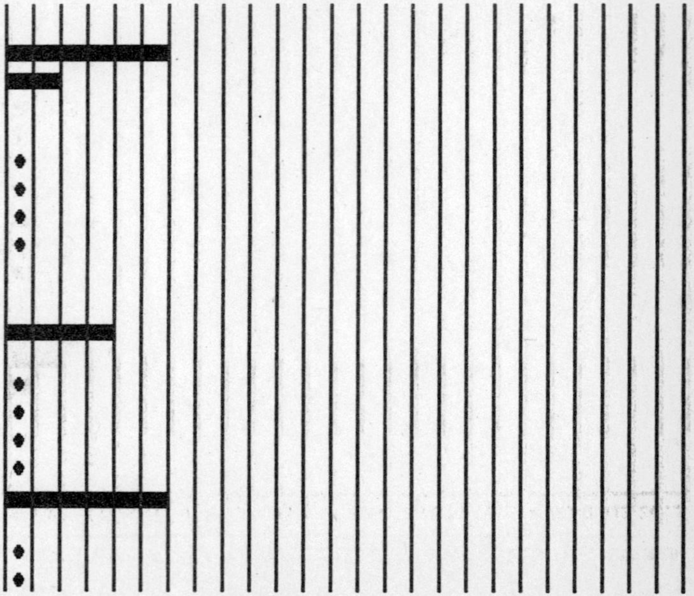

♦ = negligible

| Grams per 25g/1oz (approx) | 1 | 2 | 3 | 4 | 5 | 6 | 7 | 8 | 9 | 10 | 11 | 12 | 13 | 14 | 15 | 16 | 17 | 18 | 19 | 20 | 21 | 22 | 23 | 24 | 25 |
|---|---|---|---|---|---|---|---|---|---|---|---|---|---|---|---|---|---|---|---|---|---|---|---|---|---|
| Broad | ● | | | | | | | | | | | | | | | | | | | | | | | | |
| Butter | ● | | | | | | | | | | | | | | | | | | | | | | | | |
| Haricot | ● | | | | | | | | | | | | | | | | | | | | | | | | |
| Baked, Canned in Tomato Sauce | | | | | | | | | | | | | | | | | | | | | | | | | |
| Mung, Green Cooked | ● | | | | | | | | | | | | | | | | | | | | | | | | |
| Red Kidney | ■ | | | | | | | | | | | | | | | | | | | | | | | | |
| Bean Sprouts | ● | | | | | | | | | | | | | | | | | | | | | | | | |
| Beetroot | ● | | | | | | | | | | | | | | | | | | | | | | | | |
| Broccoli Tops | ● | | | | | | | | | | | | | | | | | | | | | | | | |
| Brussels Sprouts | ● | | | | | | | | | | | | | | | | | | | | | | | | |
| Cabbage: | | | | | | | | | | | | | | | | | | | | | | | | | |
| Red | ● | | | | | | | | | | | | | | | | | | | | | | | | |
| Savoy | ● | | | | | | | | | | | | | | | | | | | | | | | | |
| Spring | ● | | | | | | | | | | | | | | | | | | | | | | | | |
| White | ● | | | | | | | | | | | | | | | | | | | | | | | | |
| Winter | ● | | | | | | | | | | | | | | | | | | | | | | | | |
| Carrots | ● | | | | | | | | | | | | | | | | | | | | | | | | |
| Cauliflower | ● | | | | | | | | | | | | | | | | | | | | | | | | |

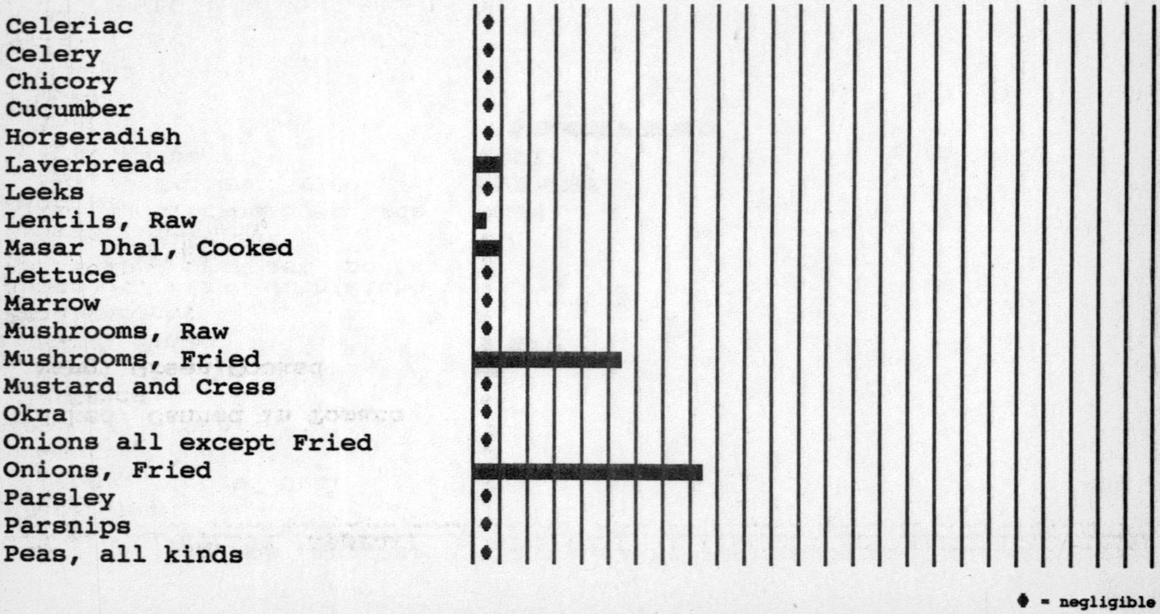

♦ = negligible

Celeriac
Celery
Chicory
Cucumber
Horseradish
Laverbread
Leeks
Lentils, Raw
Masar Dhal, Cooked
Lettuce
Marrow
Mushrooms, Raw
Mushrooms, Fried
Mustard and Cress
Okra
Onions all except Fried
Onions, Fried
Parsley
Parsnips
Peas, all kinds

## Grams per 25g/1oz (approx)

| Food | Grams |
|---|---|
| Chick Peas: | |
|   Bengal, Cooked Dhal | 2 |
|   Channa, Dhal | 2 |
| Peppers, Green | 0 |
| Plantain: | |
|   Green, Boiled | 0 |
|   Ripe, Fried | 3 |
| Potatoes: | |
|   Boiled, Baked with/without skins, or Roast, no Fat | |
|   Roast, with Fat | 2 |
|   Chips, average Home Made | 4 |
|   Chips, Frozen, Fried | 5 |
|   Oven Chips | 4 |
| Crisps | 9 |
| Pumpkin | 0 |
| Radishes | 0 |
| Salsify | 0 |
| Seakale | 0 |

Spinach
Spring Greens
Swedes
Sweetcorn
Sweet Potatoes
Tomatoes
Tomatoes, Fried
Turnips
Watercress
Yam

**YOGURT (low fat)**
Natural
Flavoured
Fruit
Hazelnut
Shape – all flavours
Shape French Style Set Yogurt
Strained Greek Ewe's

♦ = negligible

| Grams per 25g/1oz (approx) | 1 | 2 | 3 | 4 | 5 | 6 | 7 | 8 | 9 | 10 | 11 | 12 | 13 | 14 | 15 | 16 | 17 | 18 | 19 | 20 | 21 | 22 | 23 | 24 | 25 |
|---|---|---|---|---|---|---|---|---|---|---|---|---|---|---|---|---|---|---|---|---|---|---|---|---|---|
| YORKSHIRE PUDDING | | | ■ | | | | | | | | | | | | | | | | | | | | | | |

# Extra help is available

## Rosemary Conley's
## HIP AND THIGH EXERCISE CASSETTE AND POSTER

*You'll love what it does for you!*

Now you can feel fitter, healthier and even more fabulous with the fun-fitness exercise programme specifically designed to tone your hips and thighs.

This energetic but easy to follow exercise workout, to your favourite pop music, has been written and presented by Rosemary Conley. It is specially designed to tone you up as you lose your weight and inches on the Hip and Thigh Diet and will help you to keep your new trim figure toned for ever. The cassette comes with fully illustrated instructions at £5.99 inclusive of postage and packing. (UK and Northern Ireland only.)

# Rosemary Conley's
# HIP AND THIGH VIDEO

*The personal help you've been asking for!*

Rosemary Conley's Hip and Thigh Video offers personal advice to followers of her Hip and Thigh Diet. You can learn how to cut out the fat in the kitchen, how to defeat temptation and how to cope with the difficult times!

Also you can work out with Rosemary in the comfort of your own home with the Hip and Thigh Exercise Programme, specifically designed to tone your hips and thighs as you lose your weight and inches. This is the fun way to get fit and to keep your new trim figure toned for ever.

The video is written and presented by Rosemary Conley and is available on VHS price £9.99 including postage and packing. (Available in the U.K. and Northern Ireland only.)

# Rosemary Conley's
# HIP AND THIGH POSTAL SLIMMING CLUB

Rosemary Conley received many letters from readers asking for details of a club where they could find personal help and support whilst following her Hip and Thigh Diet. The Postal Slimming Club offers that personal advice and encouragement from experienced Slimming Consultants.

The initial eight-week course costs £13.99 and this can be extended to suit your individual needs as required. For further details and an enrolment form, without obligation, please write to Rosemary Conley's Postal Slimming Course, PO Box 4, Mountsorrel, Loughborough, Leicestershire LE12 7LB enclosing a stamped, self-addressed envelope. (Available in the UK and Northern Ireland only.)

...ORM

| | Quantity | Total £ |
|---|---|---|
| Audio cassette(s) and Posters @ £5.99 each | _____ | _____ |
| Video cassette(s) @ £9.99 each | _____ | _____ |
| | TOTAL | _____ |

I enclose a cheque/P.O. for £_____

Please send me details of your Postal Slimming Course

☐ *Please tick*

Please complete in block capitals:
NAME: _____
       (MR, MRS, MS, MISS)
ADDRESS: _____

_____
                    POSTCODE:
_____

Prices include postage and packing. All cheques should be made payable to Rosemary Conley Mail Order A/C. *Please write your name and address on the reverse of the cheque* and allow 21 days for delivery. Please send the above coupon with your remittance, to:

Rosemary Conley Enterprises,
PO Box 4, Mountsorrel, Loughborough,
Leicestershire LE12 7LB